Industrial Policy after the Crisis

Seizing the Future

Patrizio Bianchi

Councillor for Education and Research of the Regional Government of the Emilia-Romagna region, Italy

Sandrine Labory

Lecturer of Applied Industrial Economics and Policy, University of Ferrara, Italy

Edward Elgar
Cheltenham, UK • Northampton, MA, USA

© Patrizio Bianchi and Sandrine Labory 2011

All rights reserved. No part of this publication may be reproduced, stored in a retrieval system or transmitted in any form or by any means, electronic, mechanical or photocopying, recording, or otherwise without the prior permission of the publisher.

Published by
Edward Elgar Publishing Limited
The Lypiatts
15 Lansdown Road
Cheltenham
Glos GL50 2JA
UK

Edward Elgar Publishing, Inc.
William Pratt House
9 Dewey Court
Northampton
Massachusetts 01060
USA

A catalogue record for this book
is available from the British Library

Library of Congress Control Number: 2010939213

MIX
Paper from
responsible sources
FSC   FSC® C018575
www.fsc.org

ISBN 978 1 84980 417 2 (cased)

Typeset by Servis Filmsetting Ltd, Stockport, Cheshire
Printed and bound by MPG Books Group, UK

Contents

List of figures vi
List of tables vii
List of abbreviations viii

Introduction 1
1. The 2008 financial crisis 10
2. Globalisation and the organisation of production 40
3. Division of labour and industrial development 60
4. A framework for defining industrial policy 87
5. Industrial policies as long-term strategies: some examples 106
6. The European experience 124
Conclusions 139

References 145
Index 152

Figures

1.1	Real GDP growth of BRIC and advanced countries (per cent per year), 1980 to 2014	18
1.2	GDP level in PPP as per cent of world GDP, 1992 to 2014	19
1.3	Real GDP growth since 1980 (annual per cent change)	19
1.4	Corporate profits with inventory valuation adjustment, financial and manufacturing sectors, in billion dollars	24
1.5	Net investment in US manufacturing, 1996 to 2008	25
2.1	World merchandise exports, $ billions	41
2.2	Exports of goods, $ billions	43
2.3	Imports of goods, $ billions	43
3.1	Pin production process of a single craftsman	64
3.2	Production cycle of differentiated pins	65
3.3	Production growth by multiplication	65
3.4	Fordist production systems	67
3.5	Globalised production systems	69
4.1	The relationship between provisions and entitlements	96
4.2	Four levers of industrial development	102
4.3	The sundial of industrial policy: the EPIT framework	103
5.1	Real GDP growth in Brazil, China and South Africa, 1990 to 2012	107
5.2	Real GDP growth in Finland and Ireland, 1990 to 2012	108
5.3	Sundial showing changes needed in Chinese development	111
5.4	Sundial of Brazilian development	113
5.5	Provisions and entitlements in South Africa	114
6.1	Key levers of EU industrial policy	136

Tables

1.1	Real GDP in EU countries, 2000–11, per cent change	30
1.2	GDP per capita in the EU, EU-27 = 100	32
2.1	World merchandise exports by regions and selected economies, 1948–2008	42
3.1	Economies of scale and scope	70
6.1	Phases of the evolution of European industrial policy	134

Abbreviations

EEC	European Economic Community
EMU	economic and monetary union
EU	European Union
Fanny Mae	Federal National Mortgage Association
FDI	foreign direct investment
Fed	Federal Reserve
Freddie Mac	Federal Home Loan Mortgage Corporation
GDP	gross domestic product
ICT	information and communication technologies
IMF	International Monetary Fund
LTCM	long term capital management
MITI	Ministry of International Trade and Industry (Japan)
OECD	Organisation for Economic Co-operation and Development
SME	small and medium enterprises
UN	United Nations
WTO	World Trade Organization

Introduction

The 2008 financial crisis is significant not only from the point of view of the deep recession it has generated, but also because of the problems in the governance of the economy it has revealed. It is an extraordinary opportunity to change the governance of the economy and the way economists represent it.

The aim of this book is to reflect on the lessons that can be drawn from the crisis for the analysis, definition and implementation of industrial policy. We do not propose new rules for the economy or new forms of capitalism, but we do suggest a research programme for a new approach to the analysis of industrial development. This approach centres around an analysis of the organisation of production and stresses the importance of industrial development for the wealth of nations, taken to mean not only rising income, but also civil development (the wider goals of economic development considered by classical authors). We thus suggest that returning to a political economy framework may be extremely useful for economic analysis.

This book is not a review of the work of classical economists, which we would only perform badly because we are not economic historians. However, we use classical works in order to define a framework for the analysis of industrial policy. In this book, we define industry as the capacity to organise production, to transform inputs into outputs. We do not reduce industry to manufacturing but consider industry as all productive sectors, including agriculture, manufacturing and services. This is important not only because many goods are now bundled with services in their production (firms in the manufacturing sector extensively using business services), but also because considering all value production is important.

Industrial policy has various definitions in the literature. Broadly, two types of definitions can be identified. One is restricted and considers industrial policy as selective interventions that favour specific firms or specific domestic industries. These intervention policies generally distort competition by favouring some firms at the expense of others. Wider definitions also exist that consider industrial policy as a set of instruments promoting industrial restructuring and industrial development. Promoting industrial development supports the emergence of new industries, be they science-based or based on other types of innovations (such as new goods or new design), and helps older industries restructure.

We consider industrial policy in a broad sense, not only because it aims to correct market failures and promote industrial change, but also because it is envisaged as a strategic policy, which is essential to broader economic growth and also to social and civil development. Industrial policy is not about picking winners and protecting them so that they can be competitive. It is about defining a vision of industrial development and determining the rules and resources that can best channel this development. We thus adopt a holistic approach to industrial policy decision-making. Industrial development occurs in a complex web of interactions between different spheres of the economy. As a result of globalisation the economy has become even more complex, with firms organising worldwide production processes and interacting in a variety of ways in overlapping networks.

Industrial policy before the crisis consisted of a set of actions in various fields, including trade, competition, research and technological development, implemented at regional, national and supranational level, that provided conditions for business to prosper. The problem was that the different actions tended to lack coherence because of a lack of long-term vision. Industrial policy after the crisis primarily consists of defining this vision at the political level so that the set of actions that are pursued become complementary and integrated, putting the economy in a coherent and sustainable industrial development path. In order to define this long-term vision, a holistic approach is necessary that considers the whole system in which a particular industry or region is part. Such a comprehensive approach can identify a coherent industrial development path and the appropriate levers to promote such development.

Given this background, we argue in the book that the major implications of the 2008 financial crisis, in terms of industrial development, are for the dominant regulation model. The crisis revealed this model as inadequate to face the deep structural changes that have been occurring since the 1980s, often summarised in the term 'globalisation'.

Globalisation is not only an economic phenomenon whereby financial flows, trade of goods and services and foreign direct investment rise on a worldwide basis. It is also, and primarily, a political phenomenon whereby the bipolar world of the post-World War II era, dominated by US hegemony, no longer exists. Globalisation is clearing the scene for a multipolar world where many powers of the past return: China, India, Brazil and Russia (although the latter was, as the Union of Soviet Socialist Republics, one of the two world powers of the post-war era). China particularly is growing in strength and influence and is expected to overtake the US and become the biggest economic power within ten to 20 years[1] (O'Neill and Stupnytskz, 2009).

The emergence of new powerful economies will undermine the 'old' powers' economic dominance. More fundamentally, the rise of new powers may also lead to questions about the system of values on which the Western world is built and rooted. Democracy, respect for human rights, fair trade, health and fair standards of living for the whole population, are the pillars of the Western world.

China has a long history, a strong tradition and specific values, but the key question raised by its emergence as the biggest world power is what values it will directly or indirectly impose on the rest of the world. China has gained a strong competitive advantage essentially by maintaining very low production costs, supported by poor working conditions. As shown by Rodrik (2008), Western consumers, when informed about the labour and social conditions supporting particular goods' quality and prices, are not willing to sacrifice ethical values for lower prices. Can we sustain trade with Chinese products manufactured by workers in poor conditions with long hours and very low salaries? Taken in a broad sense, industrial policy is also concerned with these issues.

In this context, political and ethical values can no longer be ignored by economists advising policymakers. This is what Robbins was already emphasising at the beginning of the 1980s (Robbins, 1981). Industrial policy as a long-term vision of industrial development needs to ease these structural changes and make development sustainable – that is socially and environmentally coherent.

Seen as the rise of new powers, globalisation has had deep structural effects on industries. Competition has become more intense with new rivals challenging existing market incumbents. As explained in Chapter 2, this has induced production re-organisation whereby production processes have become more intensive users of intangible assets, primarily knowledge, together with the spatial fragmentation of production phases – not only between different firms, in networks of suppliers, but also between different geographical spaces, with different suppliers located in different parts of the world. The creation of 'global value chains' or 'global production networks' is a structural change that has important implications for the competitiveness of industry in different countries, and has, especially since the beginning of the century, started new debates on industrial policy (Bianchi and Labory, 2006b).

Therefore, beyond the macroeconomic mechanisms at play in the 2008 financial crisis, deeper roots can be found in the structural changes in industry over the last 20 years; changes that have not been properly addressed by the dominant regulatory model of neo-liberalism. As we show in Chapter 1, the crisis revealed that the capacity of markets to self-regulate is limited, with excessive short-termism leading to increasing stress in the world economic system, and ultimately to the crisis.

In economics, the long-term is seen as a logical time period where all adjustments are automatic, so the questions of how and when adjustment processes take place can be ignored. In fact, adjustment processes take time and involve different costs that must be examined to formulate appropriate industrial policies. Short-term macroeconomic stabilisation is not sufficient to make structural changes sustainable.

Industrial development has profound implications not only on economic growth, measured by real gross domestic product (GDP) increases and improvements in income levels, but also on the living conditions of citizens. Individuals' nature of work determines their income, their capacity to learn, their open-mindedness, and brings about social improvements; their capacity to learn determines cultural development. The fact that people learn new skills, new ways of working, get higher income, and access different types of products and services, all have social, economic and political consequences. In turn, industrial development is determined by the characteristics of societies. To give a straightforward example, in societies with strong class or ethnic divisions, where certain classes or ethnicities may be precluded from access to education or other public goods, industrial development may arise but be confined to certain parts of society and not use all resources in the country fully.

So industrial and economic development should be seen as instruments for cultural and social development, which is what classical authors such as Adam Smith had in mind. In this perspective, the current debate on justice and happiness – on what should be the appropriate measures of the development level of countries – is highly relevant. This wider view implies that the sustainability of industrial development, in the sense of social cohesion and environmental preservation for future generations, is important to take into account.

The work of classical economists is also useful to analyse the structural changes induced by globalisation, as we show in Chapter 3. The organisation of production is labour division. The division of labour depends on the extent of the market and thus upon capital accumulation. The division of labour increases labour productivity because the dexterity of workers improves, there are time savings from specialisation, and specific machinery is invented. Smith, in *The Wealth of Nations*, gives examples of the division of labour within firms but 'some of the activities which were originally a part of the division of labour within the firm may eventually become a different "trade" or "business", so that the division of labour within the firm is but a step towards the division of labour amongst firms' (Heinz and Salvadori, 2003, p. 111). The division of labour proceeds within and between firms, and in the process new 'trades' are created. New technical knowledge is constantly created and scientific knowledge is increasingly used in the production process, opening new markets and enlarging existing ones, thereby acting as the driving force of economic and social development.

The changing division of labour has deep social and political implications. The nature of work changes so that workers may have to develop new skills, particularly their capacity to communicate to others and work with others. Their status in society may also change as a result. For instance, if a large parts of workers are employed on short-term contracts rather than permanent contracts not only does their well-being change (as they face more uncertainty about their future income and cannot realise long-term plans, such as building a family) but also their social status changes. The decision of a firm to delocalise part of the production process has implications on the local community, which may find itself facing a high unemployment rate.

Thus the decisions made by firms have important social and

political implications. This fact raises two issues. First, governments should care about what firms decide and what the implications are for local and national communities. Second, firms should be viewed as political entities and not merely private players. When a firm decides to drop waste into a river near its factory it may not take the external cost of its activity into account, but it is making a political decision to ruin the local environment and adversely affect future generations.

A holistic approach to industrial policy therefore primarily addresses systemic failures in economic development, that is failures of the economic system that lead to inappropriate development paths.[2] Market and government failures are also taken into account, in that specific measures may be adopted to address specific failures of the market and to provide appropriate incentives for all actors to support the industrial strategy. However, an additional aim of a holistic approach to industrial policy is to provide coherence to the different actions implemented in different areas and at different levels, thanks to the political definition of a long-term vision, which is translated into a long-term strategy for industrial development.

The book is structured as follows. The first chapter analyses the crisis and its implications for industrial development and industrial policy. The chapter argues that what the crisis reveals most vividly is the need for long-term visions to govern the economy; that markets do not self-regulate; and that the crisis has deep structural roots and is not just an accident causing superficial injuries that will heal to leave the world as it was before.

The second chapter examines these structural changes in more detail, looking deep into the system and the organisation of production. An analysis of what 'globalisation' is and implies for industrial systems is undertaken, showing the transformation of productive organisations. The phenomenon of global value chains or 'second unbundling' in the words of Baldwin (2006) is shown to constitute one of the most important such structural changes. We relate this change to the consolidation of the knowledge-based economy and the growing importance of intangible assets. We conclude from this chapter that the economy forms a complex system where all sectors are interrelated to different degrees. The organisation of production is a fundamental aspect that needs to be analysed in order to understand this complexity and to point out where markets may not always automatically generate equilibrium.

Given these structural elements, the third chapter starts formulating a political economy framework for the analysis of industrial policy, or at least a research programme aiming at this formulation. For this purpose, we go back to an analysis of Adam Smith centred on the role of labour division in industrial and economic development, where *The wealth of nations* is primarily determined by the division of labour, in the sense of the organisation of production and the distribution of working activities between all members in a society. We argue that the second unbundling can be analysed in terms of changing labour division, extending the study made by Smith of production processes in his pin factory metaphor. We also argue that these changing production processes result from globalisation and the consequent intensification of worldwide competition, implying the necessity for a higher knowledge content of products and production processes that more intensively use intangible assets. We suggest that more research is needed on production processes in order both to define which tasks are more and less likely to be offshored, and to check whether non-'offshorable' tasks are those more intensive in intangible assets and producing more value added.

The fourth chapter consequently develops a framework for industrial policy as a long-term vision of industrial development. We show the limits of the view of industrial policy as correcting specific failures (although this is useful), essentially because this approach leads to a fragmentation of industrial policy actions without comprehensive and integrated objectives for industrial development. The approach based on systemic failures is less limited, given that development is considered as occurring in systemic and dynamic processes.

We identify four major levers that industrial policy after the crisis should take into account. These are resources (especially human capital), entitlements (rights or capabilities in Sen's wording), innovation (as a dynamic element of development) and territory (embeddedness of development processes within communities, in the sense of regional and social cohesion).[3] All these levers should be included in the long-term strategy of industrial development, at the different levels of implementation. Coherence is therefore key to defining a successful vision; coherence not only between the different areas of action, but also between the different levels of implementation (local, regional, national and supranational).

Industrial policy is then a dynamic process whereby policymakers identify possible industrial development paths and define gears and levers to orientate development in appropriate ways. The dynamics of the framework we propose in Chapter 4 is determined essentially by the learning capacity of the system, in turn determined by social mechanisms underlying work organisation and labour. Policy has an important role to play in favouring the dynamics of the system, by providing entitlements and provisions, implementing actions towards the territory (determining its capacity to valorise competencies and skills) and innovation (actions favouring knowledge creation) which all affect the individual and collective learning capacity of the system. These actions in turn influence the "skill, dexterity and judgment" of labour and the evolution of production organisation.

The fifth chapter illustrates the framework in a number of country cases, namely China (and the Shenzhen region in particular), Brazil (very briefly), South Africa and two European countries, Ireland and Finland, interesting for the very rapid economic growth they experienced in the 1990s, although with very different approaches to industrial policy. In each case the long-term vision of industrial development (or lack of) is shown, together with the main elements of the strategy, concluding with an assessment of its completeness and coherence, as well as its sustainability.

The sixth and last chapter analyses the European experience of industrial policy. It shows that the European integration process has, from its beginning, been guided by a long-term vision of industrial development where the economic integration process itself has been proposed as the main industrial policy for members of the European Community, now European Union (EU). The chapter also analyses the programme of industrial development that was proposed at the beginning of the twenty-first century in the Lisbon Strategy, and shows how it constituted an industrial policy in the sense we intend. However, the lack of political commitment that has characterised the attitude of member states since the end of the 1990s has led to the failure of the Lisbon Strategy. We conclude that the new strategy defined for the period 2010 to 2020 could, if member states truly adhered to it, constitute a new industrial policy project that, mobilises national industrial development and the pursuit of the economic integration process. However, recent post-crisis events, and in particular the attitude of eurozone countries facing the Greek crisis, raises doubts about the EU's ability to end the crisis and mobilise itself to remain a world economic power.

We therefore suggest that going back to a political economy framework which, in the words of Dahrendorf (2008), takes into account entitlements and not only provisions (see Chapter 4), would be useful to improve the capacity of economies to avoid crises. We therefore add a (modest) contribution to calls that have been made by some of the most prominent economists since the beginning of the crisis for a return to a political economy framework for economic analysis. Thus Stiglitz (2010) argues that we have to change capitalism, returning to moral responsibility, trust and collective action. Fitoussi and Laurent (2008) call for a return to a political economy framework to design sustainable economic policies. Rodrik (2008) also calls for a consideration of the political space in order to design appropriate development policies.

Our aim in this book is to relate the analysis of the actual crisis, the consideration of production organisation as central to the understanding of economic phenomena, and the role of the state in globalisation. In our view the fundamental link lies in people. In fact, in the 1990s much stress was put on the importance of knowledge in economic phenomena. What we wish to underline is that knowledge means people: people living in institutional and social contexts, that can be modified by public action either to restrict the rights and freedom or to valorise their capacities and competencies and their rights.

NOTES

1. See for example, Global Economics Paper no. 192 by Goldman Sachs (J. O'Neill and A. Stupaytska) (2009).
2. The concept of systemic failures has been defined in evolutionary theory to denote the failures of innovation systems (Von Tunzelmann, 2010). We consider here systemic failures in the whole economic system.
3. See proposed the concept of capabilities, focusing on positive freedom, in the book *Poverty and Famines: an Essay on Entitlement and Deprivation* (1981).

1. The 2008 financial crisis[1]

INTRODUCTION

The 2008 financial crisis has been a shock to many actors in, and observers of, the economy. This is not so much because it came as a surprise but because it implied a real questioning of many ideas and rules previously thought to be certain and universal, as well as a profound rethinking about the relationship between the state and the market.

The crisis is first and foremost a crisis of trust; consumers no longer having trust in the stability of the economic system. The crisis stemmed from an unforeseen collapse of the financial and housing markets in the US that spread to the whole world economy through a mechanistic reduction in the value of savings. This transformed the financial crisis into a real crisis with a negative effect on expectations and a complete stop in demand growth. The implosion of the US housing market, due to unsustainable sub-prime mortgages, led to a crisis of the banks, the dispersion of savings, a drastic fall in US demand followed by a fall in US production and a fall in US imports, causing the contagion of the crisis to the rest of the world: first to Europe and then to China and emerging markets.

The crisis saw an enormous bubble burst, a bubble created from three main ingredients. First, there was the abundant liquidity in world capital markets fed by the large payment imbalances between countries (a current account deficit in the US Fed by capital coming from emerging and oil-exporting countries) and the expansionary monetary policy pursued in the US since 2000, which kept interest rates low. Second was the credit boom, which led to unsustainable leverage (housing market). The third ingredient was financial innovations such as securitisation and derivative contracts that eased the growth in financial intermediation. The loose monetary policy conducted by the Fed led financial operators to expect a continuously accommodating policy and created prevailing expectations that regardless of mistakes or developments, financial operators would be rescued by monetary authorities. As a result speculation could continue without brakes.

The crisis led to a return of state intervention, as a guarantee against the weaknesses of the economic system. States around the world have massively intervened in markets, pouring in huge amounts of money to sustain banks. This intervention has marked the end of the liberal wave started in the late 1980s, as the ideology of laissez-faire has shown its many limits. However, this intervention is not a return to protectionism, which has many limits as well.

Beyond the dynamics of the crisis itself and the short-term reactions of states aiming to reduce its negative effects and prepare the grounds for recovery as early as possible, the deep roots of the crisis lie in the inadequacy of the regulatory model of the post-war era to deal with the new world order emerging with globalisation. These deep roots are precisely where the links between the crisis and industrial dynamics and industrial policy originate.

In the last two or three decades of globalisation, an important geopolitical transformation has occurred with new powers emerging to question the hegemony Western countries had enjoyed for the previous century and more. Countries such as Brazil, Russia, India and China (the BRICs) are examples of these 'new' powers, although 'returning' powers may be a more appropriate term as these countries have been world powers in the past. The bipolar world of the post-World War Two era has ended, leaving a multipolar world in transformation where the balance of power between countries and world regions is still in the process of adjusting and stabilising. The surprise of the crisis is that even the superpower of the post-War era, the US, has started to show not only weaknesses but also economic and political vulnerability.

The emergence of these new economic powers has had a profound impact on business, deeply changing the competitive environment and inducing structural adjustments that we analyse in more detail in Chapter 2. The current chapter focuses on the analysis of the crisis itself and on the inadequacy of the current regulatory order, about which many scholars have set out calls for change.[2]

The second section provides some considerations on both the term 'crisis' itself, in terms of meaning and supposed cyclicality, and on the major elements of economic and political evolution in the world since 1945. The aim is not to be exhaustive but to outline some of the events we find mostly significant. The third section shows the weaknesses of the US economy and the predominant role of this country in the 2008 financial crisis. The fourth section briefly examines the reaction to the crisis, mentioning fiscal stimulus measures and showing the lack of reaction of the EU collectively, although it should have constituted an example of international coordination. The fifth section shows the excesses of the neo-liberal model in terms of increasing the gap between the financial and real spheres of the economy. The final section concludes, by looking into the deeper structural changes that partly caused the crisis.

CRISES AND ECONOMIC DEVELOPMENT FROM 1945 TO 2009

Reflection on the Term 'Crisis'

A crisis is not an exceptional event, exogenous to economic development cycles, but rather it is a substantial element of structural dynamics. The term 'crisis' represents both the point at which a preceding equilibrium breaks up and the recession phase that follows. The term therefore implies separation, break, reasoning and decisions. The Greek roots of the term stress the perception of difference and the awareness of the critical moment when transformations arise. The Latin roots stress the structural break represented by the crisis, namely a moment when the phenomenon is a change of route. In the Chinese language these latter two aspects are represented in the same ideogram, which expresses the term as both a danger and an opportunity.

The term crisis has been used for a long time in the medical field, indicating the moment at which a diagnosis was made and therefore a decision was taken on the treatment to follow. The term took on a political meaning in the seventeenth and eighteenth centuries, when it was used to indicate the transition from old to new regimes, and the simultaneous existence of continuity and transformation, on the basis of a cyclical and no longer deterministic view of the historical process. The French scholar Paul Hazard showed in his book *La crise de la conscience européenne, 1680–1715* (1935), that the crisis of the Ancien régime was first and foremost due to a fundamental change in social relations, initiated by cultural transformations and intellectual thoughts that stressed rationalism, doubt, equality and freedom instead of obedience to dogma and submission to the Church and the King. Capitalism was indeed born and developed in years of a strong cultural and social break from the past.

During the expansion of capitalism the very substance of the term crisis changes. In the past, crises arose from scarcity – that is, a dramatic drop in the availability of resources due not only to land fertility problems, but also to wars or to the characteristics of the social structure. Within capitalism, the key determinant of economic development and well-being is the capacity to reproduce goods. Within capitalism, crises are therefore related to overproduction or more generally to the disequilibrium between demand and production; between the capacity of the market to create demand and the capacity of producers to respond with adequate quality and quantity of production.

Nevertheless, the economic analysis of crises still rests on the scarcity problem, as defined in the so-called marginalist revolution that spurred the creation of the neo-classical school of economics. This approach ignores the political sphere (in the sense of cultural, social and political aspects of economies), so much so that the double meaning of the term crisis disappears – crisis ends up meaning an empty moment wherein a recession phase follows a growth phase.

The use of the term crisis therefore recalls a biological, almost naturalistic metaphor, where a crisis phase is followed by a phase of regeneration and development, in turn followed by a new decline and death, which subsequently generates a new life. This metaphor, translated into economic terms, becomes an evolution following cycles. The length of cyclical phases can be diverse and partly depends on the capacity of the various economic agents to manage the crisis and so exit and recover in a positive way. The design of appropriate institutions is crucial to crisis management and achieving a positive exit from the crisis. The literature on the cyclicality of crises is wide and identifies different types of cycles, especially long cycles unfolding over the course of decades or centuries. Kondratiev extensively studied this type, identifying the famous long waves of about 50 years' duration alternating between periods of high structural growth and periods of relatively slow growth.

Kondratiev wrote his theory in 1925 (*The Major Economic Cycles*) by reconstructing the long history of capitalism from its beginning, using English price series over the period 1770 to 1920.

Schumpeter in *Business Cycles* (1939) suggested naming the long waves, 'Kondratiev waves', in honour of the economist who discovered them. Schumpeter not only recognised the importance of Kondratiev's work but also deepened his analysis by suggesting an interpretation of the different phases in the cycles. Schumpeter did this according to technical progress (unlike preceding explanations focusing on monetary factors) or more precisely, to the emergence of a radical innovation: a disruptive technology that was accompanied by numerous smaller innovations and technologies. The first wave identified by Kondratiev, over the period 1790 to 1850 is that of the cotton textile, iron and vapour machine; the second wave covers the period 1850 to about 1900 and is characterised by railways and steel; and the third wave, from 1900 to 1940 is that of electrical, chemical and automobile industries. Studies have been carried out identifying new waves – such as that of oil, automobile and mass production – in the second half of the twentieth century lasting up to the age of information technologies in the 1980s and 1990s, leaving room for a new phase after the current crisis.

Of course, the idea that the long-term evolution of economies follows cycles of a specific time period can be criticised, both because the identification of cycles is somehow arbitrary (given the many determinants of growth one can identify different cycles depending on which determinant is more strongly followed), and because the fact that some cycles have been identified in the past does not necessarily imply that a new and similar cycle will follow in the future.

However, the economic cycles defined above can be explained by specific developments. In particular, the different phases correspond to different technological developments, while the cultural, social and political contexts interact with these developments in a systemic way that slow them down or spur them on. For instance, a declining phase started in the middle of the nineteenth century, specifically in 1848 when a new wave of revolutions occurred across Europe (although they ended with the authoritarian leadership of Napoleon III), and with the first global conflict, the Crimean War, which occurred in 1856. The recession phase between 1869 and 1883 is characterised not only by events such as Italy's unification, the creation of the German Reich, the American Civil War and the Meiji revolution in Japan, but also by the colonial wars through which Great Britain and France built their colonial empires. Thus in the crisis years the new world was being prepared.

After the First World War the new world advanced in the midst of numerous tensions; the last empires ended, often in dramatic revolutions, while nation states consolidated, generally establishing authoritarian regimes that were in very delicate equilibrium. The defeated countries paid a high price for the War. The great crisis culminated in 1929, signalling a return to protectionism and even autarchic tendencies in many countries. The failure of the League of Nations is the clearest sign of a lack of collaboration and coordination between countries. All these aspects prepared the ground for a new global conflict, the catastrophic Second World War. After these long global conflicts, the world ended up strongly and neatly divided into two and supported by a very delicate equilibrium in which two coherent systems competed and excluded a third one, called the Third World, which was characterised by underdevelopment and chronic poverty.

A Brief History of Crises from 1945 to the 1980s

Between 1945 and the 1980s/the Western world consisted of the US, Canada, Western Europe, Japan, South Korea, Australia and New Zealand. The Eastern world was centred around the USSR and its satellites, with difficult relationships with China. The frontier between the two worlds was sometimes torn or kept in place through suffering, as shown by the Vietnam War or the construction of the Berlin Wall.

The implosion of the Soviet Union and the transition of many communist countries to market economies put an end to the political system underlying the global economy, opening the way for globalisation. Globalisation can be represented by a game in which all players play against each other, including new important players such as China, India, Brazil and the new Russia, so much so that it has become necessary to establish new rules for the game. The old rules of the game were established during the Second World War, at Bretton Woods. After the disasters caused by the bad rules established after the First World War, European countries had learned from their mistakes and had new ideas in mind.

Keynes, although very young at the time, criticised the rules established at the end of the First World War and reached a new conclusion in his books *The Economic Consequences of the Peace* (1919), *Tract on Monetary Reform* (1923) and numerous articles, some of which were published in *Essays in Persuasion* (1931). These thoughts led him to argue that after a very strong discontinuity such as a war economy it is not useful to try and go back to the situation that existed before, but rather it is preferable to concentrate on sustaining the economic recovery on the basis of the new conditions. In 1936 Keynes published *The General Theory of Employment, Interest and Money* and in 1940, *How to Pay for the War*. In that later small tract, he proposed compulsory savings and rationing in order to prevent inflation during the war. He was at the Treasury during the war and after thinking about measures to accompany the war economy, he focused on economic measures for the post-war era. He formulated a proposal for 'Bancor', an international clearing union, in 1943 and led the British delegation at the international conference of Bretton Woods in 1944. But his proposal was rejected in favour of a US alternative which pegged currencies against the dollar and the dollar against gold.

Keynes stressed the importance both of an active role for the state in order to sustain investments, and of international economic liberalisation, regulated by international institutions that could manage the transformation of economies. This illuminated view, however, was not accepted at Bretton Woods, where the American economy imposed itself at the centre of the new world order, with its currency becoming the basis of the international monetary system. Keynes had highlighted the risks of such a system and had proposed the Bancor as a composite currency made up of different national currencies, which would support an international monetary system based on the stability of numerous economies rather than just one.

The strength of the American economy was supported by a complex public action which had at its core the military industrial complex. Strong public spending on defence contributed to domestic demand, but the largest contribution stemmed from mass consumption and low imports. For many years this system was consolidated by the decreasing costs of both raw material and labour, labour supply being fed by immigration, in a regime of fixed exchange rates and capital costs. European countries started to grow again in the mid-1950s, thanks to the opening of the internal market within the European trade area and the common external tariff protecting European economies from US imports. This situation continued through the economic boom of the early 1960s.

All European countries, winners and losers, had to reconstruct their economies after World War Two. France, the UK, Belgium and the Netherlands also had to end the colonialism which had supported their growth prior to the war but was explosed as unsustainable in the new world order. Exports increasingly contributed to growth, first within the European Economic Community and then in the US. Japan experienced a similar history of reconstruction and economic boom.

After the 1960s, however, the international economic system based on a strong American economy started to show weaknesses as the American economy showed signs of difficulties, primarily linked to the Korean and Vietnam wars. In 1971 President Nixon declared the end of the convertibility of the dollar into gold. The long crisis that has taken place from the 1970s to the 1990s, although with ups and downs, reveals the incapacity of the system to forecast and regulate a structural break. The end of the fixed exchange rates regime, the steep rise in oil and raw material prices, the endless labour conflicts, and the high inflation that for years accompanied economic stagnation shows again, as pointed out by Keynes, the need to identify adequate levels of governance in the world economy ahead of changes that affect its political organisation.

In the 1980s and 1990s only Europe attempted an institutional innovation, by deepening regional integration to elevate collective action beyond national borders. On the other side of the Atlantic, political unilateralism was relaunched, dubbed the Washington Consensus, whereby the American economy remained the point of reference for the world order and pushed for trade opening without rules, and the rapid transformation of some countries (both in transition and emerging) to support the integration of the world economy.

The new economic phase was characterised by the collapse of communist countries, due to the inability of centrally-planned economies to adapt to the increasing complexity of the world economic framework. The bipolar world established from the middle of the twentieth century gradually faded in the two decades from 1990 to 2010, leaving room for a multipolar world characterised by a return of the Asian powers, particularly India and China. Their increasing influence is primarily due to their rapid economic growth and the rapid increase in their wealth (Figure 1.1). The influence of the US has reduced in relative terms to these returning powers, but also due to internal problems, highlighted in the next section. After a very difficult transition, Russia also reasserted itself as a world power, mainly thanks to its large reserves of natural resources, especially oil and gas.

However, as shown by Figure 1.2, the growth of China as a world

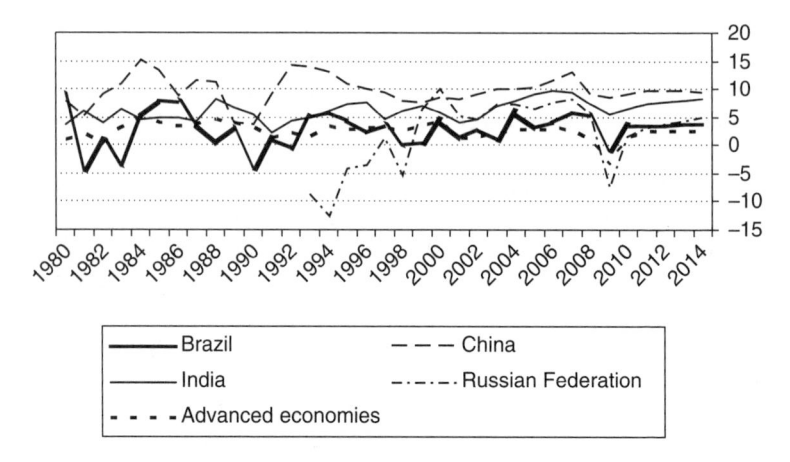

Figure 1.1 Real GDP growth of BRIC and advanced countries (per cent per year), 1980 to 2014

power, in terms of percentage of world GDP, is striking, since it is rapidly reaching the absolute level of US GDP (through not yet per capita) and seems to be heading for even higher levels.

The lack of adjustments to the world economic system has translated into various crises, that Krugman identifies in his 2008 book *The Return of Depression Economics and the Crisis of 2008*. He recalls the warning signals of crises in several Latin American countries, the Japanese and then the Asian crises, and the speculative waves that have characterised the world economy over the last years of the 1990s; all these were tremors that signalled the arrival of a bigger earthquake, the financial crisis of 2008. The earthquake is having devastating effects because the epicentre is no longer at the margin of the world economy, but at its centre, in the US economy.

Macroeconomic Evolution since the 1980s

World economic growth has experienced ups and downs since the 1980s, and the analysis of this data helps understand the roots of the crisis. Figure 1.3 shows real GDP growth for the whole world, for advanced economies and emerging and developing countries, since 1980.

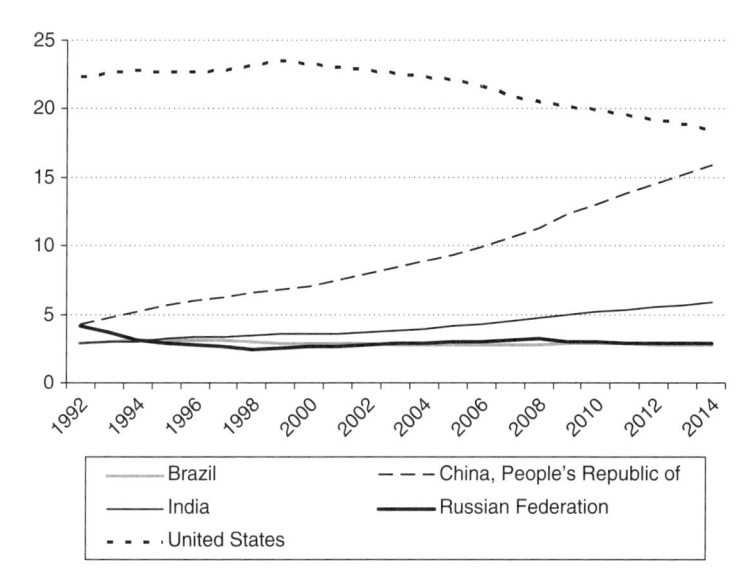

Source: IMF. 2010–2014 are forecasts.

Figure 1.2   GDP level in PPP as per cent of world GDP, 1992 to 2014

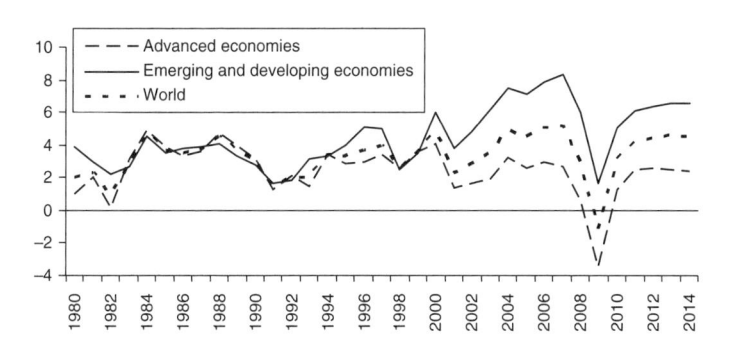

Source: IMF statistics, www.imf.org. 2010–2014 are forecasts.

Figure 1.3   Real GDP growth since 1980 (annual per cent change)

From the mid-1980s there was a first economic cycle characterised by growth up to 1988, followed by a reduction of GDP growth rates up to the period 1992–94. A new cycle followed, of accelerating growth up to 2000 (apart from the 1997 crisis), followed by a sudden reduction in growth rates in 2001, and then the actual development phase until the current crisis. The most striking point illustrated by the graph is the growing distance between emerging countries' growth rates and those of advanced countries. The latter have been hit most by the actual crisis – almost going back to the growth levels of the early 1980s. World growth is now entirely driven by the economies of emerging countries.

The growing tendency of emerging countries to drive world growth can be dated back to the early 1990s. This corresponds to the fall of the Berlin Wall and the end, from a political point of view, of bipolarism. This divergence of growth levels accelerated with the Twin Towers disaster on 11 September 2001.

Between the fall of the Berlin Wall and the Twin Towers disaster many changes occured. The EU deepened integration with economic monetary union (EMU) and the adoption of a common currency between some core member countries. Notice that European countries thereby follow Keynes's advice to base their international monetary system on a composite currency, making stability the responsibility of all members. Much has been written on the euro, some of it arguing before found that the new currency would be too weak. After its inception it was revealed to be too strong. In any case, during the current crisis the single currency has demonstrated an element of stability and strength for European countries, even though the EU is still adjusting to the most important enlargement of its history (in terms of number of new members) after the entry of Central and Eastern European countries. Of course, EMU is not without problems (Bianchi and Labory, 2009).

Such enlargement has consolidated the growth of these transitional countries, not only attracting capital from abroad, but also acquiring productive activities from Western Europe, thereby generating export economies that could restructure, and allowing the extension of supply networks across the whole European continent. The rapid growth of Eastern European countries also spurred the growth of Western ones, so that benefits were shared among old and new members of the EU.

In other emerging countries, growth was very high during the whole period, especially in China. At the end of the 1970s, modernisers led by Deng Xsiao Ping were governing the country. The policy of Deng was characterised as opening China to the world economy, attracting capital first to the area of Shenzhen between Canton and Hong Kong (see case study in Chapter 5), then to the rest of the country, basing industrial development on low cost production for the external market. This opening also produced demands from the Chinese people for greater democracy that the regime did not sustain. The Tienanmen Square slaughter (4 June 1989) made clear that the only way to support economic opening without corresponding political reforms is via high growth rates and growing incomes for the population.

Since then China has kept high growth rates, delivered by export growth and internal demand growth, together with a competitive exchange rate. In the same years, all Asian countries, except for Japan, experienced rapid growth, barring the 1997 crisis that hit Japan first and foremost.

The Japanese economy has experienced extraordinary development since 1945 based on exports and internal demand. In the 1990s, while internal demand growth slowed, exports were also increasingly rivalled by producers in other Asian countries. A stop-and-go policy was implemented to reduce inflation but also to support exports. A speculative bubble was created, which shifted savings and investments towards activities with high short-term returns, at the expense of productive investments.

Eventually the speculative bubble exploded, showing that the stock and housing markets' values did not correspond to the real economy. This resulted in huge losses for families and the banking sector, followed by a fall in consumption and industrial investment and a growing public deficit. The government intervened with strong public spending to sustain the economy, increasing the budget deficit to more than 10 per cent of GDP and debt to 100 per cent of GDP. On top of this massive action was necessary to save the banking system. The Japanese economy only recovered in 2003, thanks to growth in world demand and growing exports (of intermediary goods) to the Chinese economy. However, the Japanese economy still contains weaknesses, with an ageing population and mature industrial system.

This 'Japanese disease' has been somewhat shared in other Asian countries where rapid economic development led to the World Bank in the mid-1990s defining them as 'the Far East miracle'. In 1997 the devaluation of the Thai currency started a period of financial crisis that extended across the whole of Asia. Thailand is a small economy and very open; so much so that its recession is rapidly extended to the other Asian countries.

On the other side of the world, Latin America also experienced big trouble, again mainly due to the disparity between the financial and productive spheres of the economy. Indeed, the search for short-term profits led the financial markets to expand rapidly, attracting all savings, at the expense of the productive sectors which had difficulties in investing and the government sector, where deficits tended to increase. This disparity grew up to the point where financial assets became too overvalued and the bubble exploded.

In the same manner, in many Latin American countries, after the so-called *Decada Perdida* (last decade) of dominant dictatorships, strong inflationary tendencies strained the return to democracy. Argentina and the other countries pegged their currencies to the dollar, reducing inflation but also bringing drastic internal restructuring that forced less competitive firms out of the market in a regime of open trade and an overvalued currency. Here again a bubble in the financial and housing markets shifted resources away from the productive sectors and brought about a new dramatic crisis in 2001.

In these years the only two countries that did not experience a major crisis were China and India. India implemented a series of reforms during the 1990s that allowed the country to consolidate growth based on the development of a competitive industrial sector, supported by investment in human capital.

Various crises took place elsewhere in the world with similar scenarios to Latin America – namely the development of economic weakness accelerated by financial and housing booms that crowded out sectors of the real economy. To this one must add the rigidity of international institutions which only believed in and applied the so-called Washington Consensus. They forced a drastic reduction in the role of the state, with a reduction in interest rates, so that the capacity of the government to intervene with monetary policy was reduced. Alongside this was privatisation and liberalisation of financial markets as part of trade opening and the rapid integration of capital markets. These events were considered local, ignoring their systematic nature across different parts of the world – until they also hit the American economy.

THE 2008 CRISIS

The Problems of the American Economy

The signals of the productive crisis in the US are not recent at all. From 1991, the US balance of payments continuously and dramatically worsened, especially relative to that of China. While the balance of payments was worsening, unemployment went down from 8 to 4 per cent, essentially due to the development of tertiary activities that were seen as necessary for the American economy.

While new firms were created in new sectors, a new financial sector was also developing that brought these firms to very high capitalisation levels. The housing market also expanded greatly, with capitalisation effects similar to those of the financial sector. Financial innovations sustained a booming market and the rapid development of the tertiary sector, but this experienced its first internal crisis in 2000. The 11 September tragedy hit a US economy already in crisis, with the unemployment rate rapidly rising to above 6 per cent.

The extraordinary growth of the financial sector was not supported by a growth in the real economy, however, but by an enormous increase in public and private debt. In the private sector economy, the negative effects of stagnating wages on internal demand was compensated for by the encouragement of household debt. Innovations in the financial sector allowed financial institutions to propose and sustain loans to a growing part of the population, even those in the lowest income classes. Internal demand continued to experience a sustained growth (from $4.5 trillion in 1988, to $6.1 trillion in 1998 and $8.3 trillion in 2008, according to the US Bureau of Labor Statistics) while wages in the lowest and middle income classes stagnated.[3]

In the public sector of the US economy, after 2001 there was a strong recovery thanks to the boom in public military spending. Although the dollar was undervalued, the balance of payments kept worsening because of rising imports of consumer goods from Asia. In a situation characterised by cheap money and the boom of new financial instruments, the housing market continued to boom, incorporating the inflationary expectations of an increasingly indebted economy, in both the public and the private sectors.

This mix allowed the economy to expand thanks to the contriving reductions in interest rates and ever rising public debt. In October

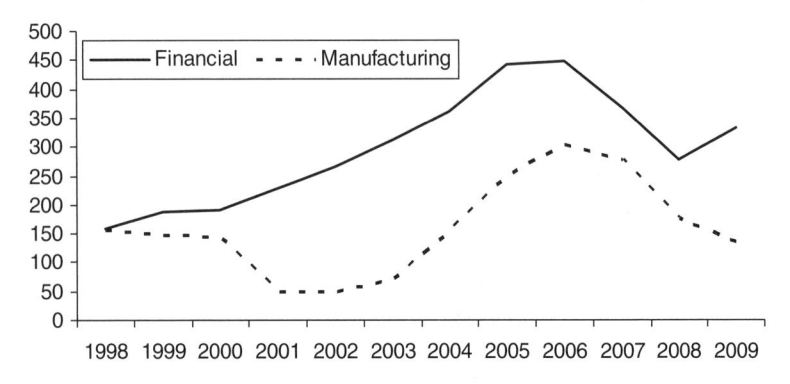

Source: US Bureau of Economic Analysis, online data, www.bea.gov.

Figure 1.4 Corporate profits with inventory valuation adjustment, financial and manufacturing sectors, in billion dollars

2008 the federal public deficit reached $10.5 trillion, rising by an average of $3.88 billion per day. This corresponds to public debt of $34,555 per capita.

The financial sector meanwhile literally boomed, as shown in Figure 1.4 by the evolution of US corporate profits in the last ten years. The trend of corporate profits in the financial sector has clearly grown, more than doubling from about $150 billion in 1998 to almost $350 billion in 2009, while the trend of corporate profits in the manufacturing sector has slightly decreased, from the same level as the financial sector in 1998 ($150 billion) to $136 billion in 2009 (Figure 1.4).

The recovery of the American economy after 2001 was therefore partly based on traditional public intervention in the defence sector. However, this increased public debt without a corresponding development in the industrial sector which faced international competition but saw financial resources dragged away, either to the military sector or to the financial and housing sectors. Indeed, investment in manufacturing fell in the mid-1990s and has remained at lower levels from 2000 onwards (Figure 1.5).

Chinese imports have been compensated by Chinese authorities purchasing American public debt, thereby allowing a dangerous liaison between the two economies. The result is a disaster. The American economy needs to be restructured, with a redefinition of the role of the state in order to base growth on healthy foundations.

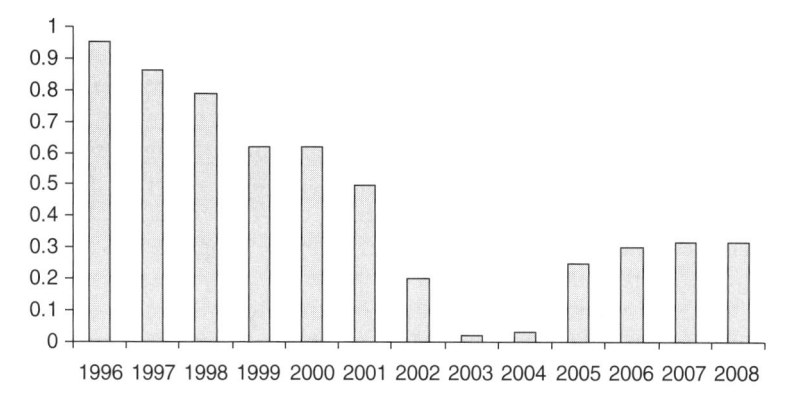

Source: US Bureau of Economic Analysis, www.bea.gov.

Figure 1.5   Net investment in US manufacturing, 1996 to 2008

Barack Obama won the 2008 election with a programme aimed at redefining the rules of the game between the state and the market, boosting internal demand through a variety of state action and forcing a restructuring of industry.

One of these actions was the proposal to re-establish the principles of the Glass-Steagall Act of 1933 (repeated in 1999), which imposed the separation of bank types according to their business (investment and commercial banks). After a lengthy process, banking reform measures were finally adopted in the US in July 2010. Known as the Dodd-Frank Wall Street Reform and Consumer Protection Act, the measures have been presented as the first major financial reforms since the Great Depression, and include new regulation on derivatives, regulatory oversight and large banks in difficulties.

A Brief Chronology of the Crisis

The key date in the collapse of US financial institutions was 14 September 2008, the day when Lehman Brothers, one of the most important and prestigious American financial institutions, went bankrupt. However, signs of the weakening of economic and financial structures had already emerged before this.

On 7 February 2007, the US Senate strongly recalled the high risk of subprimes; on 22 February 2007, HSBC Bank USA declared about $10 billion in losses; and New Century Financial went bankrupt on 2 April 2007, American Home Mortgage on 6 August and Ameriquest on 31 August. Already in that period, companies with hedge funds were quickly selling or liquidating them. In the meantime, most banking institutions in the US announced huge losses. In October 2007 the crisis reached Germany and the UK with a crisis in those banks most exposed in the US. In mid-November, Goldman Sachs estimated that potential losses from the subprime crisis were already more than $400 billion.

On 20 November Freddie Mac (Federal Home Loan Mortgage Corporation) and Fannie Mae (Federal National Mortgage Association) announced significant losses. These institutions had been two pillars of the American dream. Fannie Mae was created by Roosevelt in 1938 so that American families could afford to buy a house using loans provided by a private company but with government support (quoted on the stock exchange since 1968). Similarly, Freddie Mac was created in 1975 to guarantee the savings of American families.

On 5 December 2007, the Attorney General of New York summoned large investment banks as part of the inquiry into the securitisation of subprime mortgages. While financial institutions announced enormous losses one after the other, President Bush, who had long thought that the crisis would be temporary, had to present a plan to avoid the foreclosure of more than one million homes. Only at that point in time did the Fed implement its first action to reduce interest rates and launch new credit lines for banks at risk. On 14 December 2007, five central banks, the US Federal Reserve, the Bank of England, the European Central Bank and the national Banks of Canada and Switzerland announced that they would make $110 billion available in loans.

In January 2008, major banking institutions announced huge losses. These included Bear Sterns, Citigroup and Lehman Brothers in the US, but also Société Générale and UBS in Europe. On 13 February 2008, President Bush signed the Economic Stimulus Act providing $100 billion dollars of tax abatements and $50 billion of investment incentives. Northern Rock (a UK bank) was nationalised by the British government only three days later. On 7 March the Fed provided a further $200 billion to rescue banks while the Federal Reserve Bank of New York agreed to guarantee the operations of financial institutions and arranged the acquisition by JP Morgan

Chase of Bear Sterns, the fifth largest US bank, for $240 million. A year before, the bank was valued at $18 billion.

Among the many events it is worth noting that on 14 March 2008 Carlyle Capital, the fund linked to the financial institutions managed by the Bush family, went into default – a similar destiny to that of Long Term Capital Management (LTCM), a fund investing in high risk activities that had gone bankrupt in 1998 and was subsequently rescued. Created in 1994, LTCM had, among its board members Myron Scholes and Robert Merton who had received the Nobel prize for their studies on derivatives.

While the Fed and the Bank of England continued injecting liquidity into the system, Indy Mac went bankrupt on 13 July 2008, while Freddie Mac and Fannie Mae were rescued. On 30 July 2008, President Bush promulgated the Housing and Economic Recovery Act in order to allow the government to directly intervene in the banking system. On 5 September the Bush government nationalised Freddie Mac and Fannie Mae. On 14 September 2008, Lehman Brothers went bankrupt with $768 billion in debt. Merill Lynch seemed to be heading for the same end but Bank of America acquired it. On 16 and 17 September the government intervened to rescue AIG, the leader of the US insurance sector.

Meanwhile, central banks all around the world were injecting liquidity to sustain the financial system. The Paulson Plan was announced in the US on 19 September, creating a $700 billion fund to remove illiquid assets, but the US Congress rejected the plan. On 1 October Congress approved the Emergency Economic Stabilization Act that allowed the government to buy bad assets up to the limit of the fund.

In autumn EU governments were unable to agree on a common fund to tackle the crisis, and had to make do with the coordination of national efforts. Each European government decided on exceptional measures to rescue or sustain its national financial sector. Thus the Dutch government nationalised two major banks, Fortis and ABN Amro, in October 2008. Financial markets in Russia, Ukraine, Romania and Iceland were closed.

On 4 November 2008, Barack Obama won the US elections. On 14 February 2009, the US Congress approved an act aimed at sustaining the economy by injecting a further $787 billion into the banking system. On 30 March a plan to relaunch Chrysler was approved, while GM was subsequently rescued.

Among all the declarations that were made during these dramatic days, the most embarrassing was that of Alan Greenspan who, in October 2008, in front of a Congress Commission, admitted 'a flaw' in his ideology according to which markets always self-regulate. Many eminent scholars, such as Joe Stiglitz and Paul Krugman, had argued before the crisis that this 'hyper-liberalism' could not go on forever. The crisis seemed to put an end to it, but the difficulties in adopting measures to redefine the regulation of the financial sector, at national and global levels, has shown that the transitional phase towards a new order might be long and difficult.

REACTIONS TO THE CRISIS

Fiscal Stimulus Measures

Every country in the world implemented a fiscal stimulus package to face the crisis and soften its impact on financial and productive sectors. The total amount of stimulus in the G-20 countries was about $692 billion in 2009 (IMF, 2009), or about 1.1 per cent of global GDP. The IMF called for a stimulus of about 2 per cent of global GDP for the world economy to be effectively relaunched.[4] Within the global effort to stimulate economies, some countries have made bigger efforts. Thus the US implemented 39 per cent of the global stimulus, China 13 per cent and Japan 10 per cent. At the national level, the US stimulus amounted to about 1.9 per cent of GDP, in China it amounted to about 2.1 per cent, and in Japan to 1.4 per cent. All other countries' stimuli amounted to about 1 per cent of their GDP.

The composition of the stimuli has varied greatly across countries: some countries have almost entirely devoted their stimulus to tax cuts (Brazil, Russia and the UK), while others have almost entirely devoted it to spending (Argentina, China and India). Others have implemented it in several waves, like Germany which first implemented tax cuts and then spending. The major part of stimulus is generally composed of spending. Most countries concentrated the stimulus effort first on public consumption and transfers and second on investment. While China's stimulus was essentially focused on investment, Italy's had no investment at all and is the country with the largest tax cut on labour.

At the time of writing in January 2010 these fiscal stimulus efforts seem to have been effective in avoiding a recession across the whole world economy, although at the cost of worsening public deficits. Parallel to, or as part of these stimulus measures, some countries have had to implement some sort of national champions policy whereby some domestic firms, especially in the financial sector, have been rescued. There are positive signs that growth rates are recovering, and the main discussions on macroeconomic policies are now about the timing and extent of exit strategies and the coordination of policies among G-20 countries (Pisani-Ferry and Von Weizsäcker, 2010).

The European Union as a Prototype of International Coordination?

The financial crisis has affected Europe at a time of deep transformation. The fall of the Berlin Wall is the symbolic element of this transformation. The collapse of communist regimes opened the way to a very deep re-organisation of those economies and of the political life of those countries. At the same time, older members of the EU were pushing forward the final phases of economic integration, namely economic and monetary union, but were also reflecting on the political identity of the EU: adopting symbols and making it more democratic (through the Amsterdam and Nice Treaties).

The transition of Central and Eastern European countries towards market economies created many internal crises. Economic transition can be made rapidly but the transformation of society takes more time. Economic growth rates have varied across Central and Eastern European countries, both in levels and in times, but overall the trend has been that of a dramatic increase throughout the 1990s and through the first decade of the new century. However, all Central and Eastern European countries have been badly hit by the financial crisis.

All Central and Eastern European countries benefited, from the 1990s onwards, from their anchoring to the EU and from EU aid and support. Multinationals invested heavily in these countries, building factories that would serve the markets of the old member states but take advantage of the lower labour costs in the Eastern part of Europe. Among the multinationals investing in Central and Eastern European countries most are German. In fact, industrial production in these countries appears to be correlated with that of Germany.

Table 1.1   Real GDP in EU countries, 2000–11, per cent change

	2000	2005	2008	2009	2010	2011
Austria	3.7	2.5	2	−3.8	0.3	1.6
Belgium	3.8	2.2	1	−3.2	0	1.6
Bulgaria	5.4	6.2	6	−6.5	−2.5	2
Czech Rep.	3.6	6.3	2.7	−4.3	1.3	2.5
Denmark	3.5	2.4	−1.2	−2.4	0.9	1.5
Estonia	10	9.4	−3.6	−14	−2.6	1.4
Finland	5.1	2.8	1	−6.4	0.9	2
France	4.1	1.9	0.3	−2.4	0.9	1.8
Germany	3.2	0.7	1.2	−5.3	0.3	1.5
Greece	4.5	2.9	2.9	−0.8	−0.1	0.7
Hungary	5.2	4	0.6	−6.7	−0.9	3.2
Ireland	9.4	6.2	−3	−7.5	−2.5	1
Italy	3.7	0.7	−1	−5.1	0.2	0.7
Luxembourg	8.4	5.2	0.7	−4.8	−0.2	2.6
Netherlands	3.9	2	2	−4.2	0.7	0.6
Poland	4.3	3.6	4.9	1	2.2	4
Portugal	3.9	0.9	0	−3	0.4	0.9
Romania	2.9	4.1	7.1	−8.5	0.5	4.6
Slovakia	1.4	6.5	6.4	−4.7	3.7	5.2
Slovenia	4.4	4.3	3.5	−4.7	0.6	3.8
Spain	5.1	3.6	0.9	−3.8	−0.7	0.9
Sweden	4.4	3.3	−0.2	−4.8	1.2	2.5
UK	3.9	2.2	0.7	−4.4	0.9	2.5
EU	4	2.2	1	−4.2	0.5	1.8

Source: IMF Data Mapper, www.imf.org.

Table 1.1 shows the effects of the crisis on GDP growth in EU countries. The eurozone has been particularly hard hit by the crisis, as well as the UK. However, while the UK was expected to recover in 2011 to pre-crisis levels, the eurozone will take more time to recover. Of the four major European countries in terms of size – namely France, Germany, Italy and the UK – France appears to have been the least hard hit by the crisis, with the lowest growth level dipping to −2.4 per cent in absolute value compared to −4 and −5 per cent at the peak of the recession in Germany, Italy and the UK.

In addition, some of the EU economies that were booming prior to the crisis have also been the hardest hit. This is true in particular for Ireland, where GDP shrank by 8 per cent almost at the depth of the recession. All economies, including Ireland, were expected to recover from 2011 to pre-crisis levels, although Ireland is likely to settle down at lower GDP growth levels.

From 2000 all new EU member countries seemed to stabilise at high growth levels, without many ups and downs before the crisis. These new members are also expected to recover and to continue driving EU GDP growth during the 2010–20 decade. However, disparities are better outlined by looking at GDP per capita, as shown in Table 1.2.

While in 2000 GDP per capita ranged from about 80 to 135 (excluding Luxembourg with a very high level of 244), in 2007, after enlargement, GDP per capita ranged from 38 to 146 (276 for Luxembourg), showing a sharp increase in economic disparities within the EU. Between 2000 and 2007, most new members saw their GDP per capita rise substantially, while it remained roughly constant for old members, apart from a few exceptions such as Ireland (rising from 131 to 146) and Italy (dropping from 117 to 101).

These disparities have created difficulties for the coordination of economic policies within the EU. These difficulties were clearly apparent in the lead up to the crisis. First was the failure of the ratification of the European Constitution (with the French and Dutch voting 'no' in their respective referenda in 2005) and the very difficult ratification of the simplified Lisbon Treaty between 2007 and 2009. Second was the failure of the Lisbon Strategy that was announced in 2000 and aimed to make the EU the most competitive knowledge-based economy by the year 2010. This objective failed mainly because of the lack of coordination between national efforts and the lack of political commitment to the strategy (Bianchi and Labory, 2010). Third were the difficulties of the countries of the eurozone and the lack of coordination of fiscal policies within it (Bianchi and Labory, 2009).

The EU's difficulties reached a peak between February and May 2010 during the Greek crisis, which was ostensibly caused by the lack of solidarity in the eurozone: budget deficits and debt in the eurozone are among the lowest in the world, and certainly much lower than in the US or Japan. The main problem that the Greek crisis revealed was the lack of solidarity among eurozone members- highlighting the credibility problems of a monetary union without an underlying unified nation-state. This lack of credibility led to strong speculative attacks. Greece has a large deficit (−13.6 per cent

Table 1.2   GDP per capita in the EU, EU-27 = 100

Country	2000	2007
Euro Area (15 countries)	114	110
Austria	131	123
Belgium	126	115
Bulgaria	28	40
Cyprus	89	93
Czech Republic	68	80
Denmark	131	121
Estonia	45	70
Finland	117	118
France	115	108
Germany	118	116
Greece	84	92
Hungary	55	62
Ireland	131	147
Italy	117	103
Latvia	37	56
Lithuania	39	59
Luxembourg	245	275
Malta	84	77
Netherlands	134	133
Poland	48	54
Portugal	81	78
Romania	26	42
Slovakia	50	67
Slovenia	80	88
Spain	97	105
Sweden	128	125
United Kingdom	119	117

Source: Eurostat (www.eurostat.eu)

in 2009), but Ireland has a higher one (−14.3 per cent); yet Ireland has not been subject to speculative attack.

The solution to this crisis is not to increase the budget constraints in the eurozone by strengthening the Stability and Growth Pact even more. The main lesson from this crisis is that in order for EMU to be more credible, member states have to show more solidarity and better coordination of their efforts. The fact that EU countries took more than two months to react to the Greek crisis only illustrates this lack of solidarity. The best way of guaranteeing better coordination may be to set up a European institution, the function of which would be the governance of the eurozone and ensuring the macroeconomic stability of the EU. Increasing the European budget and making it more independent (by lowering member states' contributions and increasing independent sources such as a European carbon tax) may constitute a useful first step in this direction by allowing more European public goods to be provided. More political commitment to the integration process is needed in Europe.

Economic disparities within the EU may be a major impediment for this, all the more so as they are coupled with political and social disparities. New EU members, still in transition to democratic and market economy regimes, are experiencing deep transformations not only from an economic point of view, but also from a social, political and cultural point of view. These countries have to assert their new national identities before being able to truly commit to supranational and external constraints.

In this context, only a two-speed or multi-speed EU is possible, whereby some countries deepen some aspect of integration because they are ready and have similar development levels, while others stay out with the possibility to opt in at later stages (Prodi, 2008).

THE GAP BETWEEN THE FINANCIAL AND THE PRODUCTIVE SPHERES OF THE ECONOMY

An important effect of the crisis for our purpose is the revelation of the increasing gap between the financial and the productive sectors of the economy. The financial sector has boomed in an extraordinary manner over the last 20 to 30 years, without a corresponding expansion in the productive sphere. Thus trade on the global foreign exchange market is estimated at $3.2 trillion per day, according to the Bank of International Settlements (78th annual report, 2008). Between 2001 and 2007, foreign exchange turnover increased by an average of 18 per cent per annum, to an average daily level of $3.5 trillion, which is a bit less than Germany's annual GDP. The ratio of the volume of transactions on foreign exchange markets to world trade in goods and services was 2 to 1 in 1973, 10 to 1 in 1981, 50 to 1 in 1992 and 100 to 1 in 2006 (El Mouhoud and Plihon, 2009).

Financial flows are unevenly distributed across the world, with developed countries and especially the US concentrating a large part of these flows. Among firms, multinationals have been the dominant actors in terms of financial flows, with their global volume of mergers and acquisitions representing $85 billion in 1991, $558 billion in 1998 and $45 trillion in 2007 (according to Thomson Financial).

Financial investors are essentially institutional investors (pension, insurance and mutual funds), private equity funds, hedge funds, exchange traded funds and sovereign wealth funds. In 2008, these funds represented a value of $90 trillion, down 17 per cent from the previous year, due to the financial crisis.

Investors, especially in private equity and hedge funds, tend to push firms to increase profits in the short term. These profits are not invested but distributed to shareholders and to managers in the form of very high remuneration. Crotty (2003) estimates that well over half of the cash flow of non-financial corporations went to financial markets (in interest and dividends for example) from 1984 to 2000 (peaking at about 74 per cent in 1998). This percentage had been 30 per cent from the mid-1960s to the end of the 1970s.

The very high remuneration provided to managers in all firms, but especially in financial firms, has raised an important debate during this financial crisis. Excessive pay in the financial sector has been blamed for further pushing actors to pursue short-term profits at the expense of long-term investments. Not only do these investors push firms to short-termism, but they also create shareholdings that are no longer dispersed, as in the 1970s. Models of corporate governance have shown the advantages of the separation of ownership and control, and the superiority of a model of capitalism based on firms listed on stock exchanges rather than linked with banks or governments for corporate control and financial resources, but these models rely on the dispersion of shareholding. This dispersion no longer exists and owners have a strong influence over managers.

Countries where family ownership or state ownership does prevail, such as in Italy, appear to have suffered less during the crisis, at least in terms of the level of public spending needed to rescue financial organisations. In addition, at the end of the 1990s and early 2000s, excluding the exceptional period of financial crisis, the US Treasury has spent six times more than the French state rescuing savings banks', and the Japanese state 20 times more to saving large banks.

Hence the European model of capitalism, based predominantly

on family and state ownership (in Italy and France) or bank-firm relationships (in Germany), might have been beneficial during the crisis. In any case, the crisis made it clear that the advantages and disadvantages of various forms of capitalism must be re-examined in the current context.

In 2008 it was clear that the crisis in the subprime market in the US and the associated liquidity squeeze was having a major impact on financial institutions and banks in many countries. Bear Stearns had been taken over by JP Morgan with the help of the Federal Reserve Bank of New York, while other banks were trying to raise assets to cover their important losses: Citibank and Merrill Lynch in the US; UBS, Crédit Suisse, Barclays and Société Générale in the EU. In the UK, Northern Rock was nationalised. In Germany, IKB and Sachsenbank (state-owned) were rescued. At the end of 2008, the crisis deepened, with the collapse of Lehman Brothers.

The crisis has revealed important problems in the model of corporate governance based on the separation of ownership and control, as shown by the OECD Steering Group on Corporate Finance (OECD, 2009). Expansive monetary policies in many countries drove interest rates down, inducing investors to look for yields without paying due attention to risks. Competition in the banking sector increased and led banks to create new financial assets, such as derivatives, or to move to housing finance. Kirkpatrick (2009, p. 7) argues that 'despite the importance given to risk management by regulators and corporate governance principles, the financial turmoil has revealed severe shortcomings in practices both in internal management and in the role of the board in overseeing risk management systems at a number of banks'. Alan Greenspan himself recognised the problem when talking to the US Congress in October 2008: 'Those of us who looked to the self-interest of lending institutions, to protect shareholders' equity, myself included, are in a state of shocked disbelief'.

This problem appears to have been mainly driven by incentive systems in financial organisations that encouraged risk-taking without appropriate control by their boards. For instance, information about exposure to risks did not always reach boards and in some cases boards did not adequately monitor the activities of managers. The OECD has called for more transparent and monitored risk-management (OECD, 2009).

More generally, in financial and non-financial firms managers had too much influence on the design of incentive schemes and could manipulate them to their advantage without revealing all relevant information to their board. The OECD therefore has recommended more transparency and control in corporate governance, and a greater link between pay and performance in particular.

This lack of control of management has led to short-termist attitudes in many firms – such as looking for short-term profits and taking high risks – which has served the interests of managers at the expense of shareholders.

CONCLUSIONS

This crisis has arisen principally because of a lack of adjustment to economic and political changes occurring over the last 20 to 30 years; this globalisation has meant the end of the bipolar world in favour of multipolarity. The weaknesses of the US economy, first and foremost its enormous public debt, increasingly became vulnerabilities as its hegemony weakened in the face of other powers, primarily China, which started to finance the American economy. In the meantime, multipolarity has led to increased intensity in worldwide competition, with new rivals in markets forcing structural adjustment, quality improvement and internationalisation in firms in many sectors.

However, the dominant economic regulatory model of the last 20 to 30 years, neo-liberalism, has led to an increasing gap between the financial and productive spheres of the economy that has impeded the necessary structural adjustment, since resources were dragged away from the productive spheres of the economy to the financial and housing sectors.

These drawbacks of neo-liberalism primarily stem from its false assertion that markets self-regulate. Rather, as already stressed by Keynes, activities in the productive sphere can be hampered by excessive speculation in the financial sphere. The financial sector experienced important innovations from the 1980s onwards, inventing new financial products such as derivatives that led to high risk-taking that eventually went against the interests of shareholders and firms themselves.

The second flaw in the neo-liberal model is its short-term perspective. In fact, an important point revealed by the crisis is the importance of the long-term perspective. Firms in all sectors have to make long-term investments in order to improve processes and products.

When short-term interests prevail, these investments are no longer made, putting at risk both the long-term survival of the firm and the employees' jobs.

Long-term and broad perspectives are also necessary from a macroeconomic policy point of view. Reducing interest rates is a short-term policy that looks for immediate stabilisation; assuming that markets will self-regulate means failing to consider the long-term consequences of present tendencies. Many economists looking at the longer term, predicted that the US situation could not go on forever as it was.

In fact, we argue that globalisation, defined as the acceleration of world exchange and trade in the last 20 to 30 years, is essentially due to a geopolitical change in the world order, namely the emergence of new economic powers. This has had a profound impact on the world's competitive context. Firms in all sectors have had to adjust to the implicit or real threat from competitors located in China or in India, or in other emerging countries. The prevailing neo-liberal regulatory model turned out to be incapable of helping this adjustment, leading to crisis.

Microeconomic and macroeconomic phenomena are deeply related in the economic system. A macroeconomic policy using savings to favour investment in capital in the industrial sector has an important impact on industry. A macroeconomic policy sustaining increasing indebtedness inevitably also has a cost in the long-term. This is the third main point revealed by the crisis. Bailey and Cowling (2006) deepen this analysis by arguing that a capitalism dominated by giant corporations inevitably leads to the predominance of their interests at the expense of the interests of communities. They argue that large corporations shape consumers' behaviour by raising their propensity to consume at the expense of savings, thereby exacerbating 'short-termist pressures in capitalism, in that present needs become more pressing, and making allowance for future needs can be postponed' (Bailey and Cowling, 2006, p. 6). This is likely to have contributed to the vulnerability of the US economy prior to the crisis, by feeding the dynamics of increasing indebtedness. According to these authors, short-term macro policies are not sufficient to reduce this vulnerability. Instead, industrial policy that regulates the power of giant corporations, by ensuring that the interests of society are taken into account alongside those of elites in corporations, is key to avoid 'strategic failures'.

Indeed, the analysis of industry matters and is essential to design proper economic policies. By industry we mean the capacity to organise production in order to produce goods and services. Industry in our view therefore comprises all productive sectors, manufacturing and services together. As argued by Adam Smith, the wealth of nations is primarily determined by the division of labour that allows industrial development. The structure and characteristics of the various sectors of the economy are key determinants of the wealth of nations, as well as the interrelations between sectors. Thus a business services sector has developed extensively in the last decades, largely because manufacturing firms were changing their organisation of production and outsourced many functions that became business services. Financial services are key to the development of the economy, since they provide the necessary capital to make investment, whether in new factories or in research and development that can lead to technological progress, process and product innovations. But the rapid development of the financial sector without any connection to the 'real' sectors of the economy should be regarded with suspicion and closely monitored.

It may be that a closer look at the separate evolution of the financial and real sectors would have raised doubts and pointed to some necessary controls and regulations; but not when the dominant ideology is that markets are bright enough to self-regulate and serve the interests of the most deserving.

In our view the analysis of productive industry (all sectors, and not just manufacturing) and the design of industrial policy as a long-term vision of industrial development are essential in order to avoid crises and, above all, to ensure growth (using 'growth' in the wide sense of classical economists). This is what we aim to show in the remaining chapters of this book. In particular, the next chapter provides a more detailed analysis of the deeper roots of the crisis, namely the structural adjustments required by the changing world context of globalisation.

NOTES

1. This chapter constitutes an extension of our reflections published in Bianchi P., Labory S. (2010).
2. Many prominent scholars stress this need for change. Among these, Stiglitz (2010)

claims that 'I believe that markets lie at the heart of every successful economy but that markets do not work well on their own'. In Europe, Fitoussi and Laurent (2008) also argue against laissez-faire and propose a political economy project that would support sustainable economic development, in the sense of taking future generations into account.
3. http://www.bls.gov/emp/ep_table_405.htm
4. Http://www.imf.org/external/pubs/ft/surveys/so/2008/INT122908.htm

2. Globalisation and the organisation of production

The deep, structural roots of the current crisis lie in the extensive transformations that have occurred in the world since the 1970s. Many factors have brought about deep economic, political and social changes – primarily the oil crisis and the first crisis of the international monetary system, but also the end of dollar convertibility into gold, which showed the first sign of weakness of the world order based on bipolarism, and a crisis of the mass production system.

Consumers started to ask for more varieties of products, more care for the environment and more room for leisure, in contrast to the mentality of the post-war period up to the 1960s that was based on hard work for later pleasures. This has contributed, at least in developed countries, to a booming services sector. Advertising by large corporations has also certainly influenced this changing propensity to consume (Bailey and Cowling, 2006).

Demography in developed countries has started to change with ageing populations, implying new social security needs and new products and services, especially those related to health care and leisure. Technological progress has brought about important changes in the potential to produce and to live, from the electronics revolution to the development of the information society. Globalisation is often claimed to be a phenomenon arising in the 1990s, but it started much earlier and has been determined by many economic, technological, political and social changes.

From the 1980s onwards, the financial sector started to develop rapidly, and above all in a manner distinct from the real economy, as new financial instruments were invented enabling huge financial gains from speculation. The enabling regulatory system was a factor in its development.

The nature and extent of the market has therefore fundamentally changed. For goods, the extent of the market has increasingly become global, with firms trying to sell their products all over the

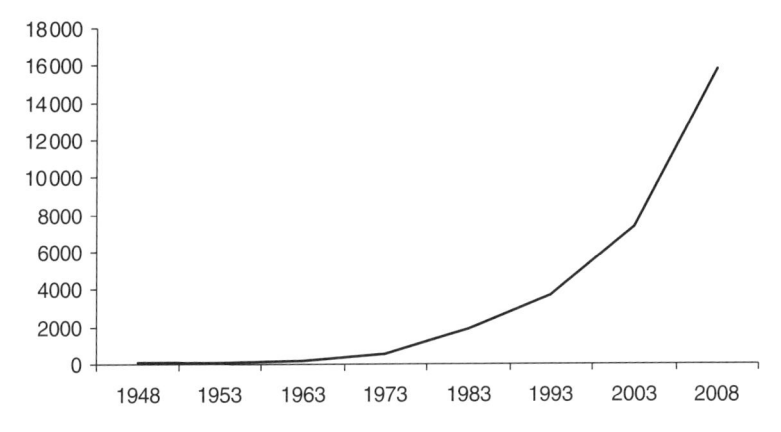

```
18000
16000
14000
12000
10000
 8000
 6000
 4000
 2000
    0
     1948  1953  1963  1973  1983  1993  2003  2008
```

Source: WTO, www.wto.org.

Figure 2.1 World merchandise exports, $ billions

world and organising production on a global scale to reap cost reductions wherever possible. The market for services has grown tremendously: services for individuals (many relating to an ageing population); business services as firms outsourced many functions to raise productivity; and financial services.

In the first chapter, we argued that the crisis is essentially due to a lack of adjustment to deep structural transformations related to the emergence of new economic and political powers (the multipolar world), and the dominant regulatory model not addressing these structural changes. In this chapter, we analyse these structural transformations in more depth and show that they imply, especially after the crisis, a need for industrial policy as a long-term vision of development.

THE GLOBALISATION PHENOMENON

Globalisation has dramatically increased the extent of the market and profoundly changed the organisation of production and the nature of work. The phenomenon can be illustrated by the graph in Figure 2.1, showing the growth in world exports in selected years from 1948 to 2008.

Table 2.1 not only shows the dramatic increase in world exports

Table 2.1 World merchandise exports by regions and selected economies, 1948–2008

	1948	1953	1963	1973	1983	1993	2003	2008
World ($ bns)	59	84	157	579	1838	3676	7377	15717
of which					Shares %			
USA	21.7	18.8	14.9	12.3	11.2	12.6	9.8	8.2
Latin America	11.3	9.7	6.4	4.3	4.4	3.0	3.0	3.8
Europe[i]	35.1	39.4	47.8	50.9	43.5	45.4	45.9	41.0
Germany	1.4	5.3	9.3	11.6	9.2	10.3	10.2	9.3
France	3.4	4.8	5.2	6.3	5.2	6.0	5.3	3.9
Italy	11.3	9.0	7.8	5.1	4.0	4.6	4.1	3.4
UK	1.8	1.8	3.2	3.8	5.0	4.9	4.1	2.9
Africa	7.3	6.5	5.7	4.8	4.5	2.5	2.4	3.5
Middle East	2.0	2.7	3.2	4.1	6.8	3.5	4.1	6.5
Asia	14.0	13.4	12.5	14.9	19.1	26.1	26.2	27.7
China	0.9	1.2	1.3	1.0	1.2	2.5	5.9	9.1
Japan	0.4	1.5	3.5	6.4	8.0	9.9	6.4	5.0
India	2.2	1.3	1.0	0.5	0.5	0.6	0.8	1.1

Notes: i: figures refer to EEC(6) in 1963, EEC(9) in 1973, EEC(10) in 1983, EU(12) in 1993, EU(25) in 2003 and EU(27) in 2008.

Source: WTO.

occurring since 1948, and especially since the 1980s (acceleration which led to the definition of the term globalisation), but also the change in participation of the various regions and countries in the world. US export share has gone down by two-thirds between 1948 and 2008, from 21.7 per cent of world exports in 1948 to 8.2 per cent in 2008. This shows the decline of the economic hegemony of the USA.

Europe's share in world exports increases over the period, but the number of countries included in the calculation changes considerably, due to enlargements of the EEC and EU. Among the biggest European countries, Germany increases its share, as do France (slightly) and the UK, while Italy sees its share significantly falling during the period. The share of Asia, and China in particular, rises dramatically from the 1990s onwards. The rise in China relative to other developed countries is also illustrated in Figures 2.2 and 2.3.

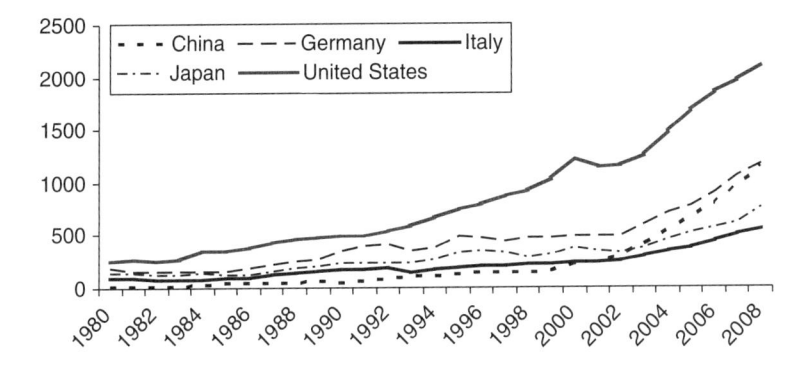

Source: Joint IMF-OECD statistics, 2010, www.imf.org.

Figure 2.2 Exports of goods, $ billions

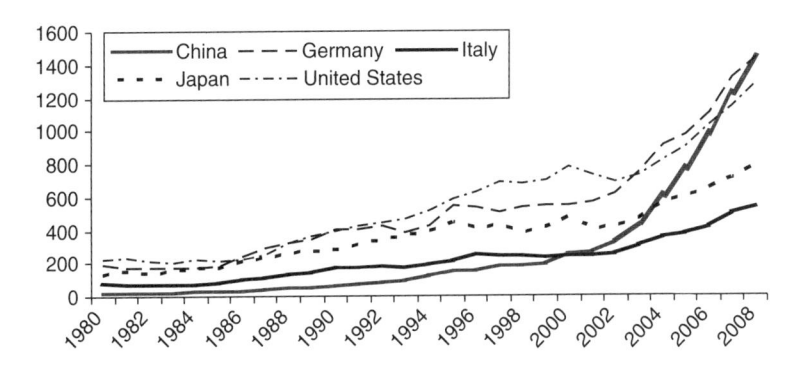

Source: IMF-OECD statistics.

Figure 2.3 Imports of goods, $ billions

China is a leading exporter but imports relatively less. In fact, the US remains the biggest importing region. This could denote increasing productive internationalisation of US firms who export some production phases abroad and re-import them to finish assembly in the home market.

The globalisation phenomenon can therefore be defined as a rapid rise in world patterns of trade in goods and services. The determinants of such a phenomenon are numerous and of different types: political determinants include the end of the bipolar world; economic factors include the globalisation of financial markets which have eased mergers and acquisitions worldwide and the setting-up of branches or factories in different parts of the world; technological factors primarily include the information and communications technology revolution which has drastically reduced communication and coordination costs across frontiers, as well as lowering transport costs.

This phenomenon is not new. It started at the beginning of the twentieth century with the reduction of transport costs, allowing large firms to become multinational firms. It has spread throughout the twentieth century, and accelerated in the last quarter of the century due to economic, financial, technological and also political factors, as the progressive liberalisation of world trade among developed countries allowed multinational firms to expand abroad.

THE ORGANISATION OF PRODUCTION AND 'UNBUNDLING'

Globalisation tends to be understood in the literature as meaning the acceleration of international trade in the last 20 to 30 years. The previous section has indeed illustrated the rapid growth of trade in finished goods and services. However, what is new in the last part of the twentieth century, and has important implications in terms of industrial policy, is the growth in the trade of intermediary products. This implies a considerable change in production organisation and a boom in productive internationalisation.

Productive internationalisation means the creation of 'global value chains' (Gereffi, 1994) whereby phases of the production process are carried out by different suppliers, and also by different countries (as the various suppliers are located in different countries of the world). Firms therefore 'unbundle' the production process, with a variety of suppliers producing parts or components for different phases of the production process. Whereas in the past such suppliers were located near the factory, global value chains suppliers are located all over the world. Some phases are made in countries where labour costs are low, others in countries where there are advantages such as high skills and competences, which make it more profitable to produce there.

The model of the large, vertically integrated firm analysed by Chandler in the first part of the twentieth century is no longer dominant, although it still exists in some sectors. From the 1970s onwards this model experienced many tensions and problems, including workers' unrest, high costs and competition from new rivals such as Japanese producers. Progressively, organisations moved towards different models. European firms first tended to prefer automation (in the 1980s), to be less dependent on workers. However, excessive automation rapidly revealed its limits, especially in the ability of the firm to adapt to frequent changes in the competitive environment. In the 1990s, the prevailing tendency of firms appeared to be outsourcing and de-verticalisation, coupled with the adoption of new work practices.

A number of empirical studies have assessed these organisational changes, using survey data which asks employees and managers how the firm's organisation is changing – for example the extent of team work, the number of hierarchical layers, compensation mechanisms, and responsibilities of the individual employee and of his team. The results of these surveys, mainly carried out in the US (Black and Lynch, 1997), in the UK (Osterman, 1994) and France (Greenan and Mairesse, 1999) is that firms tend to organise as 'network-forms', whereby hierarchical levels are few, horizontal departments and divisions are in intense communication, and teams do not only execute tasks but are involved in problem-solving. This requires workers at all levels to possess higher analytical skills, in addition to communication skills, as they have to intensively interact with colleagues in their teams and elsewhere in the firm. Higher skilled employees are favoured by these transformations since tasks for core workers with long-term contracts are increasingly non-routine, while unskilled workers are left behind: either laid off because unskilled tasks (generally, services such as cleaning) are outsourced to outside suppliers or realised in-house but by hiring unskilled employees on short-term or other flexible contracts.

Outsourcing tended to increase in the 1990s, some functions or tasks being externalised to outside suppliers in order to reduce the firm's direct costs and increase specialisation. Initially, these suppliers were predominantly located near the factory. However, throughout the 1990s suppliers were increasingly chosen in foreign countries, so that global value chains were rapidly created. Global value chains do not apply to all sectors and all firms, but the evidence is that they are spreading (Baldwin, 2006; Sturgeon, 2008).

The main factors behind their creation are falling transport costs, the IT revolution that makes coordination and communication easier and less costly even over long distances, and the emergence of new countries with potentially extensive markets. Firms established factories in these countries in order to access their booming markets and may have then discovered the feasibility and profitability of exploiting low labour costs and other local advantages – leading to the siting of specific phases of the production process there.

Although information technologies have reduced communication costs within firms organised over such a large geographical space, transport costs and coordination costs are still high, especially in an organisation based on global value chains. As a result, the theoretical underpinnings of these chains is not easy to establish (and has not yet been fully established, as stressed by Sturgeon, 2008). More importantly, the state of research on global value chains is not advanced enough to predict whether these chains will continue spreading and become a dominant production organisation mode, or whether they will remain limited to particular firms in particular sectors (Baldwin, 2006). Scholars like Yeung (2006) seem to take their spread for granted.

What the evidence does seem to show is that the phenomenon is having deep consequences on international trade, production organisation and firm competition and, as we argue here, on industrial policy as well. Baldwin (2006) makes a very interesting analysis in this respect. He defines production internationalisation as an 'unbundling', whereby phases of the production process are separated, bundled differently and carried out by different firms. Baldwin distinguishes two unbundlings. The first unbundling occurred between the late nineteenth century and the late twentieth century, as it became no longer necessary to produce goods close to consumers, thereby allowing the spatial separation of factories and consumers. Trade was consequently primarily of finished goods, and international competition was primarily between firms and sectors in different countries.

The second unbundling occurred from the last quarter of the twentieth century, as it was no longer necessary to perform phases of the production process near each other. Falling transport costs and the IT revolution (the factors favouring globalisation) allowed the spatial separation of firms' divisions and offices. According to Baldwin (2006), this unbundling occurred first in Asia because the distance between low cost countries and high cost ones was smaller. Thus Japanese firms started unbundling to low-cost Asian countries in the 1980s. In contrast, European firms intensified production internationalisation, especially after the transition of Central and Eastern European countries to market economies, moving phases of their production processes to the new EU member countries. Even Italian industrial districts moved phases of their production processes to new EU members, especially Romania, thereby deeply changing the nature of those districts. Industrial districts had been based on the separation of production phases between small and medium firms (SMEs) located in the territory, the whole being coordinated essentially thanks to shared local values and norms (social capital). Some SMEs in some districts have had to close down, replaced by lower cost foreign suppliers. Some district entrepreneurs even went to lower cost countries such as Romania in order to set up firms there that could continue to supply the district.

Offshoring has mainly affected the tasks previously carried out by so-called 'conto-terzisti', small firms focusing on simple operational tasks. It is these firms that are now disappearing from districts in Italy – only the leading firms or firms dealing with higher added value phases remain. The evolution of industrial districts seen in Italy is twofold: either an SME in the district grows to become the leader dealing with markets and governing the global value chain, or the district's firms ally with one or more leaders originating from outside the district to gain access to markets. In the first case, a district firm becomes the leader of the global value chain (Labory, 2002); in the second case, the district firms become parts of global value chains governed by external firms.

Trade no longer consists exclusively of finished goods but increasingly of parts and components – intermediary products. Baldwin argues, together with eminent scholars of international economics, that this requires a new paradigm for the discipline, where firms are no longer considered black boxes but where production organisation has to be analysed in detail to provide insights on the reasons for, and the effects of unbundling. This phenomenon also has important consequences in terms of industrial economics and policy. If competition occurs at the level of tasks, policies aiming at promoting specific firms or sectors may not be adequate. 'Picking winners' is even more difficult and useless.

Some firms in declining sectors may be doing well because they exploit good unbundling opportunities. Thus the fact that Italian industrial districts have managed to survive despite the crisis and the intense competition from emerging countries may be explained by their capacity to exploit unbundling opportunities: maintaining certain tasks in Italy while other tasks are internationalised. Generally, the production phases that remain in Italy tend to be those with greater intangible assets, such as creativity, design competence, know-how and craft competencies (Bacci, 2004).

The type of tasks that are delocalised are not homogeneous or specific. Some of them are routine tasks, requiring low skills, but some also require high skills: for example, the entrepreneur going abroad to set up a specialised factory. Some design may be carried out abroad but not all. Technicians dealing with producing machines are needed for phases done both at home and abroad.

Some scholars have analysed the type of tasks that tend to be offshored. They have found the difference is not according to the level of skills (highly skilled or unskilled labour), but according to whether tasks are routine or not. A great part of routine tasks can be codified and therefore transferred to different employees. Non-routine tasks not only involve analytical skills but also experience and tacit knowledge, which are both accumulated through time and may be transferable to new employees but at a high cost and only after some time. This does not mean that developed countries should only specialise in non-tradable tasks such as hairdressing and medical treatments. Producing goods for both the home market and foreign markets is also important for a country's economic development. However, the ability to learn and raise the knowledge content of goods, and the intensity of the use of intangible assets in the production process, are likely to make tasks less tradable. It is therefore difficult to establish with certainty which phases will be delocalised and which will not.

The unpredictability of the way in which production processes are unbundled and internationally organised is a key feature of the second unbundling process stressed by Baldwin (2006). This implies that the winners and losers of globalisation are extremely difficult to predict.

In order to gain greater insights into global value chains, more analyses of production processes and production organisation are needed in the economic literature, particularly industrial economics, in part because 'economists really do not understand the "glue" that binds production stages and tasks together' (Baldwin, 2006, p. 29).

We maintain that the way the production process is organised depends on the relative intensity of tangible and intangible assets in the different tasks. This means not only workers' productivity, but also human capital – the knowledge and competencies they bring in the production process which may not be reproducible abroad. Intangible assets also include collective knowledge creation capacities that depend not only on workers' individual human capital but also on their social capital, their shared norms and values that make communication and collective knowledge creation easier. The embeddedness of a production process in a local territory may also determine the extent of production internationalisation, since even simple tasks such as handicraft to produce leather bags may achieve higher quality and value if realised in a territory with a long historical tradition in such production. This seems to explain the interest of the highest luxury brand names such as Dior, Gucci and LVMH in the local production capacity of Tuscany's leather districts. Their know-how rooted in local culture and history appears not to be reproducible abroad, given the capacity of local workers to produce high-quality products (Bacci et al., 2010; Bacci, 2004). Bailey et al. (2010a) argue that this creates a 'place leadership' that can be maintained and extended through regional policy.

Global value chains make the traditional comparative advantage paradigm even less relevant in explaining patterns of country specialisation and for guiding policymaking. Indeed, the comparative advantage paradigm does not explain or even consider the fragmentation of the value chain in different parts of the world. Rather, comparative advantages have a different nature and are based on the capacity to create and govern global value chains.

In fact, the way global value chains are governed, as well as the place of domestic firms in them, should determine industrial policy. A country in which firms govern global value chains, shifting production according to labour costs or labour skills, will have a different industrial policy from a country where firms represent the weak links in the chain, being exposed to sudden delocalisation of the lead firm to other, more cost-effective places.

China is a place where most multinationals locate part of their production process nowadays, but the Chinese government is taking steps so that Chinese firms also become able to govern global value chains. India is also a place where multinationals locate, especially and increasingly to find highly-skilled but cheap labour, but the Indian government is not so active in supporting Indian firms to become leaders of global value chains themselves (problems in India include slow bureaucracy and continually-changing government programmes to support manufacturing such as chip manufacturing).

Baldwin (2006) rightly highlighted that the EU policy of promoting IT skills at all costs to face globalisation was wrong. Indian and Chinese workers are as able as European workers to learn those skills, and it is unlikely that these will be the less delocalised tasks. As we have argued elsewhere (Bianchi and Labory, 2004; Bianchi and Labory, 2006a, b), the knowledge-based economy constitutes an important phenomenon that has to be taken into account in policymaking. However, it does not mean a diffusion of IT across the whole society. Rather it denotes a rise in the depth of the knowledge content of products, which can be related to globalisation and the growing importance of intangible assets for countries' economic growth and development.

In the globalised economy, where competition is worldwide and intense, increasing the knowledge content of products appears to be a winning strategy. This requires new work practices, with workers made more responsible and more flexible to adapt to changes, suggest improvements, and resolve problems. Employees at all levels must be able to learn, to accumulate knowledge and to collectively create knowledge. Employees with these learning skills are probably less likely to see their tasks offshored. The literature on global value chains and firms' internationalisation shows that human capital is a key element in firms' decisions to locate in specific areas. In the knowledge-based economy, the search for skilled labour and creative capacities are central to firms' strategies.

Industrial policy must therefore look at the provision of intangible assets for firms: human capital, knowledge and innovation capacity, but also cultural and historical heritage that may at least influence consumers' perceptions of goods produced locally (again, this relates to the concept of place leadership put forward by Bailey et al., 2010a). However, not all tasks face the competition of similar task-providers in other countries. In particular, many services are not tradable because they require face-to-face interaction and the simultaneous presence of the consumer and the producer in the same place: hairdressing or restaurant meals cannot be produced at different places, and the same is true for many services such as home cleaning, repair services, entertainment and leisure activities.

UNBUNDLING AND THE GROWING IMPORTANCE OF INTANGIBLE ASSETS

Globalisation is intimately linked to the growing importance of intangible assets in economies and the knowledge-based economy. This is not taken to mean an economy where information and communication technologies operate a 'revolution', but an economy where knowledge becomes a key strategic factor. The growing importance of intangible assets has been much discussed, especially in the European Commission and the Organisation for Economic Co-operation and Development (OECD) (OECD, 2003a, b; OECD, 2001a, b; Eurostat, 2001). Their growing importance is due to many factors that can be summarised in the concept of globalisation.

As we have already argued, globalisation translates into increased competition. Products have therefore become more complex, in the sense of having higher knowledge content. They are updated more often, and consequently contain greater innovation and incorporate services. This means that the knowledge-intensive phases of production (or pre- and post-manufacturing phase), namely the research and development phase and the marketing, distribution and after sales service phases, have become more important.

Since the knowledge content of goods is nowadays higher and pre-manufacturing the key to value creation, activities carried out at these phases are very important. At the firm level, such changes have meant new forms of governance and organisation, which in fact are changes in the division of labour. In order to produce goods with high knowledge content, knowledge management within the firm becomes the key for increasing market power. In this context, the manufacturing phases of the production process become relatively less important in terms of value creation. Their only aim is to produce at lowest possible cost without leaking strategic information about the products.

The second unbundling may therefore be linked to the rising importance of intangible assets for firms, and of knowledge, since it can be considered the common denominator of intangible assets (which are primarily human capital, capacity to communicate and create knowledge, and social and organisational capital). Given falling transport and communication costs, phases of the production process that are less strategic in terms of value creation and more based on codified and easily communicated knowledge and competencies can be performed in any place. Hence manufacturing phases such as production of parts or components, or whole assemblies, have been delocalised to low cost countries.

Pre-manufacturing phases, namely research and development, and post-manufacturing phases, namely commercialisation and marketing, tend to remain in the main country of the firm. In this interpretation, the tasks that will remain in developed countries following the second unbundling will tend to be those that contain more intangible assets.

THE IMPORTANCE OF THE 'TERRITORY'

When competition primarily arises between tasks rather than between firms or sectors, the 'territory' takes on increasing importance. In this context, territories should not be seen as simple administrative units but as places where values and distinctive competencies and skills should be intensified.

One industrial policy action that has been much discussed and also concretely implemented in the last ten to 20 years is the promotion of firm clusters, especially clusters of SMEs. SMEs have become increasingly important as a result of globalisation for two major reasons. The first reason is that they have been able to take part in internationalisation, sometimes governing global value chains themselves, as in some industrial districts, or becoming part of global value chains governed by external firms. The second reason is the growing importance of intangible assets, and knowledge in particular, that make size less important and allows SMEs to be competitive. SMEs are as able to create knowledge as large firms, at least regarding non-basic knowledge creations that do not require huge research facilities that SMEs could not afford.

Clusters have been promoted because networks seem to be increasingly important in the globalised economy. As previously mentioned, not only have SME clusters such as industrial districts shown to be potentially successful production organisation modes, but also large firms have tended to decentralise internally and organise as networks both within the firm (the different units that constitute the firm are in network relationships rather than hierarchical ones) and outside the firm, setting up network relationships with suppliers which are often SMEs.

In fact, networks are effective forms of governance in the intangible economy because they allow the creation and exploitation of complementarities between holders of intangible assets in production processes. Unlike physical capital, intangible capital is difficult to acquire. In particular, individuals holding human capital (intelligence, the ability to communicate and so on) and knowledge (acquired through education and personal experience) cannot be bought and owned by the firm. Complementarities have to be created so that incentives are provided to individuals to work within the firm, through remuneration and human capital improvements prospects.

Networks are not only created between firms but also between firms and institutions, such as government agencies, local authorities, research centres and universities. In the globalised, knowledge-based economy, knowledge and intangible assets are constantly created and renewed and therefore universities take an active role in the production process. Not only do they transmit knowledge to students and hence human capital useful for industrial development, but they also take an active part in knowledge creation, through close relationships with firms. Hence networks are key in the globalised economy, and a focus of industrial development policies has been to favour the creation of clusters.

In the context of the new trade in tasks, territories are important because task specialisation primarily arises at that level. Setting up clusters where firms from any sector and any competency can form may not be useful. Rather, favouring the specialisation of clusters, in the sense of task specialisation, may be a useful element of industrial policy. This task specialisation may happen through a self-selection process, driven by market transactions and historical relations, as in the case of many industrial districts in Italy.

Task specialisation may also be induced from above. The French policy of 'competitiveness poles' is an example. The central government has made large funds available to finance the development of local clusters particularly in, but not limited to, high tech sectors.

Firms, research centres, universities and local governments have gathered to identify the products or tasks on which a cluster could be built and could competitively expand. The resulting poles are sometimes specialised in specific sectors but also on specific tasks or generic technologies at the research and development level of the production process: for example, Lyon Biopole is specialised in vaccines and diagnostics, while the 'aerospace valley' covers the aerospace sector but specialises in specific phases of the production process (research and development and manufacturing).

DEVELOPMENT IN THE GLOBALISED, KNOWLEDGE-BASED ECONOMY

Trade in tasks therefore appears to strengthen the role of the local or regional level in industrial development. Trade in tasks implies that is it possible to spur industrial development by strengthening the relationship between innovation promotion, growing productivity and firms' networks.

Task specialisation cannot be successfully imposed from above, from a central government that would apply fashionable strategies or recipes already experienced in other contexts. Rather it depends on the more or less recent history of a territory: on its social structure, the economic organisation and the effective institutional governance of the territory. These factors combine and produce a unique situation that has to be governed with specific instruments which may have been used in other contexts but which have to be applied with originality and creativity as well as an awareness that instruments operate within a specific social structure, made up of different people, many of whom are able to express a public 'voice'.

The objective of policymakers is not to apply abstract models, but to define a holistic approach to development which combines available resources with social objectives, sometimes learning from policies experienced in other contexts. When the social objective is to increase citizens' quality of life, the process by which this objective is reached is as important as the final result.

In this context, SME policies can have different meanings: either acting as an instrument of technology diffusion that can imply rising productivity of the whole system, or as actions allowing the largest possible share of people to take part in economic activity.

It is necessary to adopt a complex vision of development, where various actions combine in a long-term perspective to stimulate different agents to follow a balanced and sustainable development path. Economic dynamics are rooted in social and local contexts, and become active when the context is open and able to adopt innovations without disaggregating. It is not enough to identify the strength of local communities as a common language and shared values and norms. The dynamic aspects of social structures must be able to transform without losing identity but rather by adapting identity and governance.

In this sense, this complexity must also involve the definition of industrial policies that can accelerate economic innovation processes without breaking the social context. The need for this unitary vision of industrial policy interventions also give rise to the consideration of the side effects of specific actions on other parts of the economy, as well as a reflection on the links existing between different parts of the economic structure.

For example, a policy promoting the development of high tech small firms simultaneously requires actions that favour a general increase in the productivity of the economic system, and the support of SME networks that allow collaboration and synergies between different SMEs in shared innovation projects. Without these simultaneous actions, the risk is that SME policy has a limited impact on the local economy: a policy favouring spin-offs from universities will not impact regional development if the regional industrial context does not have sufficient endogenous development capacity.

Thus an Italian region like Emilia-Romagna, in which industrial development was previously based primarily on industrial districts in traditional sectors, has completely redefined its industrial development policy by putting these two aspects together: favouring innovation and spin-offs from universities, and favouring the adoption of new technologies by existing firms by creating a dense regional network between local authorities, firms, universities and other research centres. Without this global long-term vision, clustering policies incur the risk of being limited in scope, which does not help exploit the tendencies for structural change stimulated by opening processes.

Clustering can be a solution to the risk inherent in any innovative activity, given that the vulnerability of small firms is compensated by the variety of firms located in the territory. However, various factors determine the growth of such small, innovative firms and all factors have to be taken into account in cluster policies. In addition, cluster policies should also pay attention to the diffusion of the knowledge created in clusters to the rest of the economy. Otherwise the policy risks generating a gap between protected high tech zones and zones dominated by firms with low competitiveness relative to foreign competitors. The policy also risks generating a gap between social groups in dynamic clusters and other social groups somehow left behind, as shown by the recent social unrest in the high tech cluster of Grenoble in France.

Clustering policies should also pay attention to competition. A risk indeed exists that local collusions or new dominant concentrations could be favoured in order to face international competition. Today, monopolies of information and knowledge can create dramatic constraints in industrial development and democracy.

We believe therefore that task specialisation primarily arises from the bottom, namely from local or regional contexts, but which have to be combined in a wider frame at national or higher levels (as in the EU). The delicate interconnection between local experiences can only function if, simultaneously, conditions of effective competition are created. In other words the actions favouring the growth of new competitive subjects must take into account the international competition context and curb the monopolistic temptations of economic actors.

GLOBALISATION AND INDUSTRIAL POLICY: NATIONAL OR REGIONAL LEVELS?

Since the 1990s, many scholars have argued that the region is increasingly the right level for industrial policy action because industrial development is generated from the bottom. Globalisation has reinforced this view. In an increasingly integrated world, the role of the nation state is being reduced as more and more regulation and global public goods have to be defined at an international level. This is increasing the role of international institutions. The primary role in spurring industrial development comes from the regions, given that agglomerations and exchange of knowledge, as well as interest coherence, primarily arise at that level. Ohmae (1995) argued that the region-state is the appropriate level of economic analysis in a globalised and borderless world. The liberal policies implemented by most national states before the 2008 crisis reinforced this view, with the nation state appearing to surrender control by letting the market play by itself.

However, this view ignores the polity in which firms operate, still defined mainly at the national level.

Many industries have strong networks of SMEs but they are also dominated by major transnational firms that control global distribution markets (film and fashion, for example). The strategies of large firms often shape the strategies of small innovative firms in their industry networks, the regions in which they are located, and in local labour markets (Bailey and Cowling, 2006).

Policies aimed at upgrading SMEs and creating poles of excellence are useful in the open, knowledge-based economy but they also need to take account of the power relations that are established between firms. Networks are often dominated by large firms or other specific players that may take disproportionate advantage of the network's activity and then leave it further down the line.

Multinationals have considerable power to shape local labour markets. They define strategies at all government levels to construct markets and production spaces that reduce risk and increase their profits. Firms, especially large ones but also smaller ones, lobby governments to influence policymaking and public good provision in their favour.

Firms are not only private agents; they are also political agents and this should be taken into consideration in discussions of industrial and economic development. Adam Smith recognised this political nature of entrepreneurs. The degree and nature of competition is not only determined by purely economic factors (such as industry structure and firm strategies) but also by political factors such as their ability to influence market regulation.

As we previously highlighted, policies that have tried to foster industrial development, especially at the regional level, have aimed at favouring networks and the emergence of clusters. Universities are also playing a role by promoting the creation of spin-offs that ascribe value to university research. However, these policies should also aim at favouring firm growth and the emergence of leaders. Otherwise regional experiences will not make an impact on the wider regional economy. Universities have a role in favouring firm creation in high tech sectors, but they also have a fundamental role in providing an appropriately trained labour force for firms.

A key issue concerning the relative roles of the national and the regional level in industrial development is therefore determining the appropriate dimension of regional clusters or poles of excellence. In other words, determining the critical mass for development needed to make an impact in the long term on the region's and the nation's industrial and economic development. Local experiences in development are useful, but they risk remaining local and of short duration if they are not included in a wider regional or national strategy of industrial development that favours the exploitation of synergies, be they spillovers or externalities, between territories. Territories which pool experience may also be stronger in the face of dominant business players that may otherwise influence local markets in inappropriate ways.

Small may be beautiful, but sometimes the only solution for small firms to survive is to ally with large firms on which they become increasingly dependent and which may appropriate their knowledge and capacities to leave them as simple task executors. Small firms based in territories that are backed by strong industrial development policies may have greater power in international networks, especially when access to finance is made more difficult by the high internationalisation of the financial sector.

The profits gained by firms as a result of offshoring production phases to low-cost countries, have not been invested in long-term growth perspectives, but have been given to shareholders in the form of dividends (Millberg and Winkler, 2009). In fact, the pressure of the financial sector on the real sector to increase share profits may have even pushed firms' productive internationalisation in some cases, since these operations allowed an easy and rapid increase in profits.

The result is that the gains from productivity increases have not been shared with employees. In fact, many employees lost jobs as a result of offshoring, while profits were distributed to managers in the form of stock options. If this is the case and offshoring is driven by short-term profit maximisation rather than by a long-term strategy of concentrating tasks where relevant competencies and knowledge are dense, then the long-term effects of offshoring may not be positive for a country's industrial and broader development. Profits should be invested in research and development, in product and process renewal, and in employee training for the long-term prospects of the firm.

Regional development studies have included the dynamics of

complex production networks in their analysis in recent years, moving from the earlier focus on endogenous regional assets, such as human capital and social capital. The relationship between globalisation and regional change has thus been more directly examined. One interesting conceptualisation is that of 'strategic coupling' (Coe et al., 2004; Yeung, 2006), indicating the connection between lead firms governing global value chains and regional economies. The idea is that although endogenous factors are still important, they are not sufficient for regional development: external links are also fundamental, especially in the globalised economy. Hence the capacity of regional firms to set up their own global production networks or take part in one global network, by 'strategically coupling' with external lead firms, appears to be key to regional development. According to these authors, regional institutions have a role to play in favouring this strategic coupling in order to spur regional development, by stimulating processes of value creation (providing appropriate training of human capital and promoting start-up firms, for example), enhancement (technological and knowledge transfer) and capture, at different levels of government (local or territorial, regional, or national), each level acting in complementary way to the other.

Coe et al. (2004) and Yeung (2006) only seem to consider the case where firms in the regional economy relate to an external lead firm; however, strategic coupling may also include a case where a regional firm sets up its own global production network by strategically coupling with suppliers in different parts of the world. The way in which government at different levels (especially regional of course, but also at national and local levels) can promote the development of regional firms' own global production networks also appears to be interesting to explore further, especially given our word of caution regarding firms' entry into global production networks governed by foreign firms which tend to have high bargaining power. Favouring the creation of their own global production networks by regional firms may be a preferred route to avoid the dependence of regional development on foreign firms which may decide to end the relationship as soon as strategic coupling with other regions of the world appears to be more interesting.

Looking deeper into production processes and firm organisation should provide further insights on these issues. This is what the next chapter starts to do, by providing a framework for analysis.

3. Division of labour and industrial development

In this chapter, we start presenting a framework for the definition of industrial development policy. We have shown, in the previous chapter, the importance of the analysis of production organisation in the study of the determinants of industrial development and the wealth of nations (viewed as wider than economic wealth, and intending social and environmental sustainability). Production organisation has changed dramatically, with the unbundling of the various phases of the production process and the creation of global value chains. Parts of the production process can be carried out by suppliers spatially separated, even in different countries.

Production organisation was analysed by Adam Smith as the division of labour, giving rise to the modern firm. We extend the analysis of labour division to the evolution of production organisation in the twentieth century and up to today. We do not pretend to re-interpret Smith or to provide an exhaustive account of his ideas; rather, we use some of his ideas to provide the foundations of our framework for the definition of industrial policy. Note that Bianchi (1981) already used a framework based on the work of Adam Smith to explain the dramatic changes in production organisation that arose in the 1970s and 1980s, especially in the automobile sector. We extend it to explain changes arising since then.

In our view, the essence of the firm is the division of labour, namely the coordination of specialised skills and competencies of different individuals, in a dynamic and complementary manner, since skills and competencies are not static but constantly evolve through time, as individuals learn through experience. We contrast this analysis with theories of the firm existing in the literature, in order to highlight the distinguishing feature of our framework.

We conclude by deriving the implications of this analysis on industrial policy in broad terms, which will be explored in greater detail in the next chapter. The main conclusion is that industrial policy is first and foremost a process, made up of a variety of instruments combined to orient industrial development.

AN ANALYSIS OF LABOUR DIVISION

We prefer to start our analysis with production. That is, from the moment at which organisational processes aimed at transforming some (tangible and intangible) inputs into (tangible and intangible) goods that can be sold on markets are created. These processes are realised by using knowledge, capabilities and intelligence to generate value which lies at the core of the production process. This capacity to generate added value – to combine knowledge, skills and competencies and transform them into goods – is where the essence of the firm lies and is, according to Smith (1776), what determines the wealth of nations.

In other words, the determinants of economic development are not only the raw materials or the land which a territory has at its disposal but also the individual and collective capacity to transform inputs into outputs; the capability to learn and apply new knowledge to production processes; the competence to accumulate, transfer and organise knowledge and incorporate it into goods.

Smith grounded his analysis of economic processes into social and political processes. Thus, in a primitive society one produces for oneself, for one's own survival. In the feudal society one produces not only for oneself but also for the owner of the land (a Lord), who guarantees protection in exchange. In such a context the control of the land, commercial routes and raw materials, are essential to political control.

The industrial revolution drastically changed this scheme based on the poverty and ignorance of land workers and craftsmen to produce goods for the rich owners. The industrial revolution stimulated knowledge and the use of competencies in production as fewer farmers and more workers had access to a minimum education and higher income. Industrial development is thus intrinsically linked to cultural and social improvements: 'The greatest improvement(s) in the productive powers of labour, and the greater part of skill, dexterity and judgement with which it is any where directed, or applied, seem to have been the effects of division of labour' (Smith, 1776. p. 13).

Improvements in labour productivity depend on the division of labour, that is the capacity to divide an activity, a work or a process into phases on which specific knowledge or better 'skill, dexterity and judgement' is applied. The capacity to manage intangible factors is thus the key element in assigning value to tangible goods. In other words, knowledge applied to production is the engine of the production process and the value of the creation process.

The Basis of Productive Efficiency

Smith explains how the application of the skill, dexterity and judgement of workers to labour division implies an increase in labour productivity in the following way:

> 'This great increase of the quantity of work, which in consequence of the division of labour, the same number of people are capable of performing is owing to three different circumstances; first, to the increase of dexterity in every particular workman; secondly, to the saving of the time which is commonly lost in passing from one species of work to another; and lastly, to the invention of a great number of machines which facilitate and abridge labour, and enable one man to do the work of many' (Smith, 1776, p. 17).

In other words, labour productivity depends on the capacity of individual and collective learning applied to a productive process. The productive process is not fixed in time but rather constantly changes through time as learning takes place and improvements can be made. Being applied to a specific task, such as a manual activity or a study field, dexterity rises both because discernment rises with experience and study, and because one can realise the same task in a shorter time, reducing lead time and transforming some parts into a routine. A learning process thus emerges thanks to specialisation, which implies a rise in productivity. Specialisation also allows for the reduction of lead time since the same individual does not have to spend time shifting from one task to another.

In this manner the division of labour is a fundamental determinant of the wealth of nations. This has been translated, in mainstream theory, into productivity (total factor productivity) determining economic growth (namely, GDP growth). However, as previously outlined, Smith's vision was wider than economic growth. In any case, this reasoning can be applied to the analysis of production organisation not only at the time Smith wrote, but right up to today. Some broad tendencies of productive organisation have emerged in certain periods of time, corresponding to dominant production processes: the Taylorist and Fordist production processes which dominated for about a century up to the 1970s; the flexible production system designed by engineer Ohno of Toyota from the 1970s to the 1990s; and most recently the modular production system and global value chains where labour division arises not only between firms in the same territory but also between firms in different spatial locations.

The first crucial problem for a rational labour division is the identification of productive phases, where coherent learning processes can be developed. These phases should be neither too wide, where the knowledge base would be too broad for specialisation to take place, nor too narrow, where specialisation would be too 'easy'. However, specialisation also implies the need for coordination mechanisms, because when all workers specialise in specific tasks these tasks have to be coordinated. Specialisation must therefore be accompanied by a collective complementarity, meaning not only complementary tasks but also complementary learning processes, allowing the production process to be managed in a coherent manner and thereby avoiding the waste of time and of knowledge.

Specialisation and complementarity therefore represent the basis for productive efficiency, because they allow a coherent development of knowledge and the progressive reduction of the time needed to realise the whole production process, as well as the capacity to generate both new processes and new products.

The division of labour therefore generates a new phase or a new function which is implicit in craft production, namely production organisation and management. A new position emerges in the firm which is the production manager, who is in charge of dividing the production process into tasks and coordinating the whole production process. This function has increased in importance as capitalism has developed, often at the expense of individuals' learning capacities.

Production Organisation

We go back to Smith's famous metaphor, that of the pin factory, in order to explain how the widening and deepening of labour division implies changes in production organisation and the emergence of new productive functions.

If pin production was carried out by a single worker, as in craft production, the worker would take the raw material, raw metal, and would transform it through successive tasks into the final product, a box of pins. Thus the craftsman would heat the metal, make it take the shape of the pin, add the pinhead, finish the pin, wash it, put it into a box, and close the box when it is full. Some of these phases are inseparable, others are separable and can be done at different times. For instance the shaping of the pin is inseparable from the heating of the metal, otherwise one has to wait for the metal to get hot again in order to finish the shaping. Putting the pins in the boxes can be done later, independently of the shaping phase. The craftsman working on his own must stop the production of pins in order to spend time putting them in the boxes.

When the craftsman wishes to produce more boxes of pins, he can either spend more time working and produce one box after the other, or ask another craftsman to work in parallel, carrying out the same phases as he does to obtain a box of pins. Alternatively, he can divide the production phases between him and the other craftsman, with one of them making all the pins and working the hot metal while the other worker specialises in box production. This production process is summarised in Figure 3.1. First, when the same worker carries out all the production phases, he must do them in sequence, first heating and working the metal, then stopping to produce the heads, followed by another interruption to make the boxes.

The pin production process can be divided into 12 phases: wire-drawing, wire-straightening, cutting, pointing, pinhead making, pinhead finishing, pinhead and pin assembly, finishing, washing, making boxes, box filling and box closing, leading to the final product. The craftsman sequentially realises all the phases.

Raw materials	1	2	3	4	5	6	7	8	9	10	11	12	Finished product

Figure 3.1 Pin production process of a single craftsman

Division of labour and industrial development 65

```
A: RM1 ─────► 12  FP
B: RM1 ─────► 12  FP
```

Figure 3.2 Production cycle of differentiated pins

The first means to increase production is to add a second craftsman who produces other pin boxes using the same process. This new production cycle would be as in Figure 3.2, where the two craftsmen are indicated as A and B.

This can be called production growth by addition, where cycles add to each other. All craftsmen work separately, in parallel. Another means to increase production is to organise and divide the tasks involved between the two workers, A and B. For instance, worker A specialises in the production of pins while worker B specialises in making and filling the boxes. This is production growth by multiplication, because the increase in dimension changes the production cycles (Figure 3.3).

Workers A and B can work in sequence or work simultaneously: worker A prepares the pins and worker B prepares the boxes, which will be filled and closed once a sufficient number of pins has been produced. The cycle can be divided between more workers who may be able to work simultaneously. Phases 1 to 4, however, have to be realised in sequence, because they have to be performed when the metal is hot. The sub-cycle of making pinheads (phases 5 and 6) can be done in parallel, as can the sub-cycle of producing boxes (phases 10 and 11). Phases 7 and 12 are important because they concern assembly (pin and hat, and then pins and boxes). Some phases may also be improved using machines.

If production must be further increased, it is necessary to understand how much time is required for each phase in order to ensure continuity of the production cycle, thereby avoiding a worker in a successive phase waiting for the preceding phases to be completed.

A	1	2	3	4	5	6	7	8	9			
B										10	11	12 Finished product

Figure 3.3 Production growth by multiplication

The main risk is demand, which may reduce. This implies a slow down or halt to the whole cycle because all workers are now integrated in a single production process.

Labour division therefore implies the creation of a new position in the organisation: someone must look for the best ways to organise production, and must therefore dedicate his/her time to production organisation. This requires identifying the production phases and organising them into sequence or in parallel, according to whether they are separable or not.

Scale Economies

The result of this organisation is that with the same quantity of work one can increase final production. In other words, productivity can increase. All this reasoning of course assumes that demand increases so that the additional production finds a market. The division of labour therefore allows for the creation of scale economies.

The first scale economy is related to the capacity to learn. By repeating the same tasks, by working the same raw material, or by using the same machines a learning process is created using the advantages of experience: repetition creates a learning process whereby the same operations can be carried out in a shorter time. These economies of scale can be called dynamic economies of scale because they are related to the capacity to accumulate knowledge through time.

Labour division also allows the production of more in the same time period, exploiting technical knowledge at its best, producing more at a given point in time with the same inputs: these are static scale economies. The risk of labour division and specialisation is that demand changes making production capacity redundant. This risk is particularly acute when the production capacity in place does not easily have alternative uses.

Labour division always implies, to a certain degree, sunk costs because the production process requires investment in specific machines, in specific personnel training, and so on. The implication is that when a production process has to be changed these costs cannot be recuperated, as new machines must be produced and new training must occur.

A historical case of a production cycle based on static scale economies is the Fordist production system. In this system the production

Phases	1	2	3	4	5	6	7	8	9	10	11	12	Finished product
Workers	A	B	C	D	E	F	G	H	I	J	K	L	

Figure 3.4   Fordist production systems

process was divided into very elementary tasks to be performed in sequence (Figure 3.4), each worker specialising in a specific task.

As in the pin case, the product itself was extremely simplified and standardised, in order to allow the extreme labour division. This is the famous example of the black Ford T model.

With this production organisation is associated a particular firm structure: the large, vertically integrated firm. It is characterised by a high hierarchical level, the top of the firm making all decisions, communication flows being uni-directional from top to bottom (the U-form of Chandler (1962)). The associated nature of work is low skill, with elementary tasks performed by workers with few learning possibilities.

In order to see how the labour division can evolve, and how it has actually evolved, let us imagine a change in demand. If society changes so much that consumers would prefer pins with varied colours, or varied metals composing it, the production organisation shown in Figure 3.4 can be altered to meet the needs of consumers. A new production line using a different metal can be added. Different production lines producing differently coloured pins can also be added. The product is differentiated but the production cycle remains the same. The economies of scale of the production cycles are still exploited, but a new type of economy is added, namely economies of scope. This was the production organisation introduced by General Motors in the 1920s, which allowed for differentiation between the cars made while still reaping economies of scale.

A different firm structure is associated with this new production organisation: the M-form. It is still a large, vertically integrated firm, organised into divisions dealing with different products or different geographical markets, each repeating the whole production process in different geographical markets. However, with product differentiation other production phases appear related to research and development, management of the single divisions, and coordination of the whole organisation, as well as marketing and commercialisation.

As differentiation increases, the pre- and post-manufacturing phases, essentially research and development and marketing-commercialisation, become more and more important, as the work to be done becomes relatively more strategic than the work done. Smith indeed defined these two concepts in the example of black cloth production. 'A public mourning raises the price of black cloth (with which the market is almost always understocked upon such occasions) and augments the profits of the merchants who possess any considerable quantity of it. It has no effect upon the wages of the weavers. The market is understocked with commodities, not with labour; with work done, not with work to be done' (Smith, 1776, p. 76).

In case of unexpected changes in demand, it is necessary to be able to alter production. For this purpose, it is not sufficient to think in terms of manufactured goods, namely of work done, but also to manage resources and competencies that cannot yet be forecasted, namely in terms of work to be done.

Globalisation increases competition and creates the need to frequently innovate products and personalise goods. Actual manufacturing, work done, becomes relatively less strategic than the work to be done: namely the know-how and competencies to create and produce goods and services, the content of which depends on the ability to incorporate technical, organisational and market knowledge into production. The most valuable capital of the firm increasingly becomes the capacity to combine skill, dexterity and judgement in an organisation capable of operating in terms of work to be done. In other words, the most valuable capital of the firm is intangible, and based on knowledge.

The flexible and modular production processes developed from the 1980s group production phases into modules, each dealt with by a specific team with the intention to increase the capacity of the firm to frequently create and renew products, thanks to an ability to manage the work to be done.

The second unbundling can also be interpreted in this perspective. It means pushing the logic of the greater importance of work to be done to an extreme. Indeed, pre- and post-manufacturing phases of the production process are so important that they (generally) remain under the direct control of the company, in the home or main market. They can also be carried out in different divisions, located in different countries, but in a limited and controlled network. The manufacturing phases, that is assembly, are strategically less

	R&D	Manufacturing	Marketing and commercialisation	
Phases	i ii iii	1 2 3 4 5 6 7 8 9 10 11 12		Finished product
Localisation	Home or in controlled network	(partially or totally) offshored	Home or in controlled network	

Figure 3.5   Globalised production systems

important so they can be offshored to other countries where labour costs are lower. In this sense, offshored tasks are more likely to be those less intensive in intangible assets. This is, however, a hypothesis that requires empirical verification.

The new production process can therefore be represented as in Figure 3.5.

Scale Economies and Innovation

As previously mentioned, there are different types of scale economies.

1. The first type is related to the capacity to learn: to accumulate experience through time, to transfer knowledge on productive functions, so as to reduce the time to produce a good (lead time). This is a dynamic scale economy.
2. The second type concerns the ability to produce, in a given time period, large volumes of homogeneous goods, by rationalising the productive cycle, often simplifying the product, so as to reduce production unit cost. This is a static scale economy.
3. The third type concerns the ability to derive scope economies by combining the production of different varieties of the product in the same production cycle.
4. Another type of scope economy can also be outlined, namely the ability to accumulate experience and knowledge so as to continuously change the final product using the same production cycle, in order to adapt it to changing consumer needs. This is a dynamic scope economy, which is very important because it allows a firm to make product innovations while avoiding the problem of irreversible sunk costs associated with specific production process.

Table 3.1 Economies of scale and scope

Types of economies	Scale	Scope
Static	1	4
Dynamic	2	3

We can therefore summarise the facts just derived about the organisation of production in Table 3.1.

Different advantages exist for scale and scope that lead to varied production organisations. These diverse production organisations are not always substitutable, and the question now arises as to what factors drive the adoption of one form or another.

MARKET POWER, MOBILITY AND STRATEGY

Production decisions must take not only demand characteristics, but also rivals' decisions or expected decisions, into account. Smith expresses this problematic in the following way (Smith, 1776, p. 31): 'as it is the power of exchanging that gives occasion to the division of labour, so the extent of this division must always be limited by the extent of that power, or in other words by the extent of the market'.

The division of labour is therefore crucially determined by the characteristics of the market, namely demand and competition. The 'power of exchanging' in Smith refers to market power, in other words the firm's position relative to rivals. If the market extends, as when different countries initiate an economic integration process, the power of exchanging changes because demand suddenly widens and new rivals have to be considered in the wider market, with the same or different products, and lower or higher prices. We can therefore call the set of all agents that interact in a market, including consumers and producers, as well as all the agents interacting in the production of a given good, the extent of the market and their power relations, market power.

Barriers to entry can affect the number of agents interacting in markets. Industrial economics has extensively analysed structural and strategic barriers to entry, as well as firms' strategies to extend market power.

The role of the entrepreneur is therefore not only to guarantee continuity in the productive cycle between complementary phases but also to organise and manage the cycle given his knowledge of the market: that is, all agents' interactions that determine his market power. His functions therefore become more numerous and generate a new possibility for labour division within the management function. The productive cycle contains knowledge not only about the transformation of raw materials, but also about the final product and the market, namely consumers and rival producers. Management implies production organisation and planning as well as the definition of market strategies, in the sense of strategies aimed at maintaining and developing market power.

Thus as the production cycle becomes more divided and more complex, producing more differentiated goods, many additional functions are created: production planning and organisation, research and development to foster product innovation, logistics and acquisition of components, marketing, finance and so on. The phases carried out do not only regard production (manufacturing), but also pre-manufacturing (research and development, production planning) and post-manufacturing (marketing and commercialisation). All these phases represent the value added chain, by which the entrepreneur creates value added from raw materials and components by applying learning and knowledge to the production of goods and services.

The organisation that makes up the management of all these functions needed to carry out all the phases becomes a firm. A firm manages and carries out all the phases of the value added chain. In craft production, all these functions are performed by a single person. As the firm grows, labour is increasingly divided among the various phases. As the firm grows larger the necessity to separate management and ownership increases. Problems of corporate governance thus arise.

Functions that add to the pre- and post-manufacturing phases, such as research and development, marketing and commercialisation can be called strategic phases. These strategic phases have various articulations and configurations depending on the extent of the market. For instance, a firm producing a homogeneous good in a monopoly regime does not need marketing or advertising. A Fordist firm does not need to continuously market new products since the factories are specific to particular models and cannot be easily changed, but consumers only require standardised products at the lowest possible costs. In contrast, a firm producing highly differentiated products in a very competitive context will need a strong marketing department that will identify changes in consumers' tastes and advertise the companies' products, as well as a research and development department that continuously develops new products to meet the new potential demand.

The extent of the division of the value added chain into phases, and the manner in which these phases are managed within the firm, therefore determines a wide variety of possible firm organisation models. This depends on whether the firm carries out all the production phases, or concentrates on certain phases with suppliers carrying out other phases. One can also imagine an extreme case where a firm concentrates on strategic phases only, while all productive phases are carried out by other firms and suppliers.

One can also imagine a case where phases or groups of phases are managed by different firms that coordinate their activities not through hierarchical control but through market relations, and where the product of one firm is the component used by another firm. This case is characterised by the coexistence of many SMEs, which remain efficient only if conditions of specialisation and complementarity are maintained between them. This is the case of industrial districts or, more general, SME systems or networks.

Are there preferred organisational models? In other words, given demand and industry characteristics, is there an optimal organisational model for the firm? The predominance of the large, vertically integrated firm managing mass production models for almost all of the twentieth century led many scholars to answer positively to this question. But this model started to enter a crisis in the 1970s for many reasons including workers' conflicts, changing demand and changing raw material prices. The rising performance of Japanese producers in the 1970s and 1980s, together with their particular organisation model – based on just-in-time, constant improvement and modular production – led many scholars to think that a new organisational model was diffusing worldwide and proving to be optimal (see Labory, 1997, for a review).

However, the coexistence, not only across industries but also within industries, of different organisational models has led many analysts to the conclusion that the reality is one of variety and there is no dominant organisation model.

PRODUCTION ORGANISATION, INSTITUTIONS AND FIRM STRATEGIES

We mentioned above that firms choose the division of labour in order to fit products with the extent of the market. However, the specific form of labour division varies across firms and territories. Indeed, the firm's environment simultaneously shapes its strategies and labour division choices. Besides the extent of the market, the environment is made of other relevant markets and firms (suppliers), customers, the legal and regulatory context, and political and social norms. In other words, the environment is also shaped by institutions.

As stressed by Roberts (2004), strategies are implemented through organisational design, and strategic capabilities are embedded in organisations. However, organisations cannot be changed as quickly as strategies. When the environment or the extent of the market changes, the firm's strategy can be changed relatively quickly through a decision by the managers, but the implementation of the new strategy generally requires organisational, that is labour division, changes. New product characteristics may change the production process; teams may have to change, hiring new personnel who will take time adapting to the firm and integrating into it; knowledge and competencies required to perform work may change, and employees will take time learning the new knowledge and acquiring the new competencies. So two firms, adopting similar strategies in similar environments and market extent, may have differing performance if they differ in their ability to change their respective organisations to implement the strategy.

THEORETICAL APPROACHES TO THE FIRM

Economic theory has amply and deeply studied the firm, its nature and organisation. We provide here a brief review of the main theories of the firm, hopefully highlighting the main points of the different approaches. We do not aim to be exhaustive but rather to stress the main elements that appear as contrasting or as complementary to our approach. Our aim is to suggest that the existing theories of the firm are complementary and could be unified in a view of the essence of the firm as labour division.

Coriat and Weinstein (2010) argue that there are two main approaches to the theory of the firm: the contractual approach and the evolutionary approach. These approaches developed after 1970, when the Walrasian model of the firm, which saw it as a black box that combines inputs to produce outputs, was criticised. In such a model, the firm's internal organisation does not matter since markets instantaneously provide all the information necessary for decision-making, and the behaviour of individuals (entrepreneurs and consumers) is guided only by the market. Coase, in his seminal work entitled *The Nature of the Firm* (1937), argues that market transaction costs increase when information is imperfect and asymmetric. The firm is constituted in order to reduce these transaction costs. The role of the firm is then to exchange information in contracts through a strategy, a learning process, and the management and organisation of contracts.

Williamson, one of the founders of the new-institutionalist school, bases his analysis on the hypotheses of opportunism and bounded rationality, which leads to the vision of the firm as a set of contractual competencies. The firm exists because it can reduce the costs of transactions performed on the market. The firm and the market are therefore viewed as two different solutions to carrying out exchange. The heterogeneity of organisational forms (internal and external to the firms, quasi-markets, and so on) is explained by the different levels of transaction costs to be minimised.

Neoclassical View

The neoclassical view has been enriched by the introduction of information economics into models, especially the two major problems of asymmetric and imperfect information, namely moral hazard and adverse selection. The firm has information that the worker cannot completely verify before starting to work in it (its working conditions), and the worker has information that the firm cannot fully verify before he starts work (his knowledge and competencies). Incentive contracts allow the resolution of these information asymmetries in that they get the parties to reveal the information they hold. The same is true of the relationship between the firm and its suppliers or its clients. Thus, all economic activities can be reduced to exchange and to contracts. The firm is just a set of contracts. This theory assumes that each individual maximises his own interest, and does not care for the interest of others unless he is compensated for it. Only well-defined contracts can resolve conflicts.

The pioneering work on information symmetry in the theory of the firm came from Alchian and Demsetz (1972), who developed team production theory, and from Jensen and Meckling (1976) and Fama (1980) on agency theory. Alchian and Demsetz considered in particular the free-riding problems arising in joint production, and showed that team work is optimal in the case of joint inputs and a non-separable production function (when the marginal productivity of a factor depends on the quantity of that factor and of other factors). According to these authors, the firm is a set of contracts that manages team work. In other words, the firm exists because of the complementarity between production factors. Coordination problems in the firm only amount to problems of team coordination. Agency theory instead considers the firm as a set of incentives: the firm defines contracts that align the interests of its members, given information asymmetries and self-interested agents. Coordination is therefore reduced to a problem of motivation. Agency theory also examines the organisational form of the firm: its hierarchy and internal labour market.

The neoclassical theory however does not consider the existence of authority within firms. A behaviour cannot be imposed on workers and employees, only contracts can induce them to behave in a way that is appropriate to the firm, because they provide them with adequate rewards. Hence the internal labour market is really a private market, governed by economic rules and not administrative rules.

The neoclassical analysis of the firm is not limited to incentives. Other aspects studied include the financial structure of the firm and corporate governance problems. Another important question which is examined is that of information flows within the firm, and the optimal hierarchical structure that balances information acquisition costs and the benefits of rapid decision. For example, Geanakoplos and Milgrom (1985) interpret information cost as a delay in decision-making and derive an optimal hierarchy. Other studies highlight the trade-off between delay in decision-making and quantity of information processed.

Transaction Cost Theory

Like the neoclassical theory of the firm, the theory of transaction costs (Williamson, 1975, 1985) takes exchange as a unit of analysis.

The main hypothesis is bounded rationality: that is, individuals are not able to possess and use all relevant information for their economic decision. The consequence is that agents do not maximise but instead make and correct errors in order to improve their situation. This trial and error process depends on their past experience. The second major hypothesis is opportunism: that is, the search for one's own interest even at the expense of other agents.

Given uncertainty and information asymmetries, market transactions are costly and it can be convenient to adopt another form of exchange, namely a governance structure different from that of markets. The firm is then the place where transaction costs are, under certain conditions, minimised. The heterogeneity of organisational forms is explained by the fact that the optimal governance structure of transactions depends on the characteristics of transactions and on the institutional environment. Hence firms in different industries (with a variety of products and production systems), in diverse countries or regions (with different institutional environments) will adopt different organisational forms.

In other words, the firm is neither a production function nor a private market; it is a hierarchical way of governing transactions. The firm is still a set of contracts, but of a different nature than in neoclassical theory, in that contracts allow for the establishment of long-term relationships but also authority in relationships. Transaction cost theory, like neoclassical theory, is fundamentally static: given technology and market conditions, there exists an optimal organisational form that maximises efficiency (transaction cost minimisation in transaction cost theory; profit maximisation under incentive and productive constraints in neoclassical theory). The deterministic models used in transaction cost theory somehow contradict the hypothesis of bounded rationality. Williamson (1998) justifies this paradox by the fact that the analytical framework of maximisation is easy to use and reaches the same conclusions under the hypothesis of bounded rationality as under the hypothesis of rationality. The fact that both hypotheses lead to the same conclusion may not be so well-founded. One can see this very simply when considering the fact that bounded rational individuals make errors, while rational individuals do not. The possibility of errors implies the possibility for inefficient organisational forms to remain in markets. However, according to Williamson in the long term both hypotheses lead to the same results.

In both these approaches exchange is the unit of analysis and markets are the key institution to study in economics. Industrial policy is justified only by market failures.

Individuals are rational in the long-term, so policymakers do not have to care about the restructuring of productive sectors that could be brought about by shocks: in the long term, only the most efficient survive and industries will specialise in their comparative advantages, given the stock of resources available in the country.

Evolutionary Theory

The evolutionary theory of the firm focuses attention on learning and considers that the nature of the firm lies in learning and knowledge accumulation. Contrary to the previous approach, it is dynamic. Organisational competencies are the essential assets of the firm and are progressively built over time.

As Coriat and Weinstein (2010) show, the evolutionary theory of the firm is made of different approaches, the coherence of which has to yet to be more precisely found. This view was initiated by the work of behaviourists such as Cyert and March, and also Penrose who showed that the firm does not only manage information, but is also a set of resources that must be made productive in order to increase the performance of the firm. The evolutionary theory made important contributions to this view, considering the firm as a set of knowledge and competencies, with its unit of analysis being knowledge. Wernerfeld (1984, p. 172) explains that 'a firm's resources at a given time could be defined as those (tangible and intangible) assets which are tied semi-permanently to the firms'.

Coriat and Weinstein argue that what is important for Penrose is not so much the presence of resources but rather the *service* that the resource can render. The capacity of the resource to provide a service depends on the organisation and management of the firm: 'Strictly speaking, it is never resources themselves that are the "inputs" in the production process, but only the services that resources can render' (Penrose, 1959, p. 25). Firm performance depends on its capacity to accumulate resources and make them productive. This capacity in turn depends on the core competencies of the firm.

Overall therefore, the firm is either seen as a set of competencies (Foss, 1997), a depository of knowledge through routines (Nelson and Winter, 1982), a learning organisation or a problem-solver (Marengo, 1992), or a set of capabilities (Rumelt, 1984; Foss, 1997).

Like new-institutionalists, scholars of this theory consider rationality to be bounded, essentially because the heterogeneity of behaviours observed in the real world could not be explained otherwise. With the unit of analysis being knowledge and not exchange, production and innovation problems are fully accounted for in the theory. This has two major consequences. First, the competitiveness of firms is determined by their capacity to learn and create knowledge, and industrial policy can favour firms' competitiveness. Second, conflicts of interests are ignored, so that (internal or external) labour markets are not considered (Coriat and Weinstein, 2010). The way in which individuals are coordinated and motivated within firms to collectively create knowledge and competencies is not considered in detail.

Regarding the first aspect, the nature of the firm is essentially to learn and accumulate knowledge, which translates into individual and organisational competencies that determine the competitive advantages of the firm. These organisational competencies or capabilities translate into routines that represent the distinguishing features of firms, and are at the origin of their differences in performance. According to Cohen et al. (1996, p. 683), 'a routine is an executable capability for repeated performance in some contexts that has been learned by an organisation in response of selection pressures'. Routines are coordinated, repetitive sets of organisational activities.

Cohendet et al. (2010) claim that the concept of routine has to be made more precise in this theoretical approach: its origin, definition, and measurement are not clearly defined. One avenue for increasing its determination may be through deeper analyses of the division of labour processes. Learning primarily arises at the individual level, and firms combine the knowledge of different individuals by allowing them to interact and thereby share knowledge and collectively create new knowledge, the essential purpose being to integrate this knowledge into production processes.

This approach thus seems to implicitly recognise that the division of labour is the essence of the firm. Thus Grant (1996) argues that 'without the benefits from specialisation there is no need for organisations comprising different individuals' (p. 113). Organisations have to coordinate these specialisations and provide incentives to cooperate, through incentive mechanisms such as compensation and/or through authority by which the firms' managers impose specific behaviours. Individuals can bring knowledge and competencies to the firm if they have previously been able to increase their human capital through education, training and social policies. Infrastructure such as transport and telecommunications is also important to ease interactions between individuals and match them with particular needs in firms. Therefore, the state has a role to play in the provision of public goods and actions, allowing the knowledge base to increase (through research and development and education) and easing interactions (through networking).

Industrial policy is therefore dynamic and aimed at favouring the development of competencies so that existing firms can develop new comparative advantages and new firms can be created. This view stresses the knowledge content of production processes and is very close to our view, where the firm's essence is labour division to allow the specialisation of individuals, together with their coordination to ensure complementarities between specialised knowledge and competencies.

Firms learn and innovate in a context that constantly evolves, due to changes in firms' strategies (reorganisation, product innovations, and so on) and also to changes in the competitive context (for instance, the emergence of new competitors like China and India in the late 1990s). Therefore, the market and competition do not represent adjustment mechanisms but rather dynamic forces that bring about change and thereby generate conflict and instability, not harmony and equilibrium (Burlamaqui, 2000). One of the main objectives of industrial policy is thus to accommodate change and reduce uncertainty. As stressed by Burlamaqui (2000), these unstable dynamics require the presence of a robust and active state that implements both broad and selective policies to stabilise the system.

Institutions therefore matter. Chang (2000) defines the main elements of an institutionalist theory of industrial development. This theory views the market as one of many institutions that organise economic activities. Other such institutions include firms and the state, which create the rules of economic interactions and ensure their implementation.

The neoclassical theory accounts for the state as an institution, but views it as an organisation made up of self-interested individuals whose interests have to be aligned through appropriate incentives. The state is thus reduced to a 'quasi-market' and its relationships with other institutions are reduced to contractual relations. Chang rejects the hypothesis according to which the market is central in the analysis of economic activities in general, and industrial development in particular. Markets do not appear naturally but through a political process that defines the rights and duties related to the market. According to Chang (2000), politics is not a quasi-market process whereby material benefits are exchanged for political support.

When the unit of analysis is exchange and all economic phenomena can be analysed in terms of market (or non-market) transactions, industrial policy is reduced to ensuring that the market works properly. This leads to an analysis in terms of 'failures', which we will examine in more detail in the next chapter.

INDUSTRIAL POLICIES IN A POLITICAL ECONOMY FRAMEWORK

The two approaches to the theory of the firm we have presented in the last section appear to be complementary approaches in order to explain the second unbundling. First, the contractual approach is useful to address the problems of coordinating conflicting interests and the problem of motivation of a firms' employees. However, in this approach the analysis of the production process, its separation into phases, and the rationale and effects of carrying out the phases within single firms or across firms, is not considered. More precisely, the division of phases among the firm and its suppliers has been considered in these approaches but only as market transactions that in some cases (for instance, in the presence of asset specificity) are better performed within the firm itself. Second, the evolutionary approach is more dynamic and has the advantage of accounting for the specialisation of individuals into specific knowledge areas and competencies that are put together within the firm, the essence of which is the creation of knowledge.

In our view, these two latter aspects are important and should be simultaneously taken into account. The essence of the firm is labour division in order to produce goods more efficiently and to reply to market changes more effectively. Labour division in fact requires two elements:

1. Specialisation and complementarity: specialisation in specific knowledge and competencies, that allows the employee to learn and to perform tasks better (in a dynamic process).
2. Coordination of individuals with different knowledge and

competencies: the firm is made up of individuals with different knowledge and competencies who have to be motivated and coordinated for the whole to become more than the sum of the parts. Compensation mechanisms motivate individuals to apply effort and to cooperate; organisational structures allow specific forms of interaction, by specifying teams and other communication channels (such as cross-functional communication and reporting to different firm members) where individuals interact.

The analysis of the previous sections has, in our view, four main implications:

1. The centre of analysis should be the organisation of the value chain – which is to say the division of labour – not the market. The market is important in determining the possibilities for labour division but the key determinants in industry development are labour division and the organisation of the value chain, which determines the frontier of the firm and the relationships of the firm and its environment, its strategies and performance.
2. Industrial policy is aimed at promoting and easing the transformation of production organisation to meet new needs and requirements arising from change that may be political (the end of war or dictatorship), social (May 1968, the evolution of the role of women in society, or the arrival of immigrants), scientific (technological progress) or environmental (climate change being a prime example).
3. Industrial policy is a key policy for three major reasons: first, it concerns value creation, since we consider industry as all productive sectors; second, it directly impacts on a country's economic growth; third, it directly affects the standards of living of citizens. It affects their income, their cultural evolution (including education and training, and the possibility to access cultural developments) and their social status.
4. Industrial policy has effects only in the very long-term. Just as firm strategies are quick to change but not the organisations that implement them, industrial policy aims at providing new impetus and levers for the mechanics of the industrial development process to take a specific path. Industrial policy only makes

sense in the long-term, which is a problem when policymakers are concerned about voters and tend to have only the next election as their time frame. In this sense, a long-term vision such as that defined by the EU in the Lisbon Strategy can be useful because it thinks about the long-term future without too many short-term electoral constraints (see Chapter 6).

A policy aimed at developing new sectors means not only trying to base economic development on new technologies and high potential industries, but also bringing about a social and cultural evolution in society. The education system must be oriented towards more training of engineers and scientists; the population must have high skills; and as a result there will be new demands on living environments, access to culture, and so on.

Neoclassical theory suggests that providing an optimal allocation of resources implies reaching the 'best' situation for society, where each individual consumer cannot be made better off in terms of preferences and budget constraints. However, it may be that an optimal is reached but with some people not allowed access to education and cultural development. It may be that they find jobs but are unable to live in decent conditions: for instance, an individual making a living on short-term contracts cannot make long-term plans and has difficulty in accessing credit for buying goods such as houses. It may be that he contributes to the employment rate, but can that be an economic objective? Classical economists such as Smith stressed that industrial development aimed at reaching the 'wealth of nations', which meant not only higher GDP and income, but also justice and happiness, or, in the words of Sylos Labini referring to Smith, 'civil development'.

The importance of cultural development is underlined in Smith in his analysis of the division of labour. Smith expects that extreme division of labour may lead to alienation, which can, however, be prevented by education (Smith, 1776).

By sustainable industrial development we therefore mean industrial development as a support to civil development: meaning cultural and social development on the one hand, and attention to the environment on the other hand. Environmental concerns were nonexistent at the time classic theorists wrote, but the concept of civil development in a modern setting must include this aspect.

Sylos Labini (2006) emphasised this point, claiming that 'the nexus between economic and civil development is always strong, even when economic development damages civil development' (p. 105). Research is, in this respect, important not only for economic development but also for civil development, because research simultaneously results from and feeds cultural growth, raising practical issues that translate into intellectual issues.

Economic development is a complex phenomenon, dependent on political and social aspects and not just economic ones. The organisation of production has dramatically changed since the 1970s but economics has continued to be based on the same paradigm, that of the large firm realising economies of scale. New approaches have been developed since the 1970s that take account of some aspects of the new forms of production organisation, such as the analysis of districts and their external economies, together with the great importance of their social embeddedness. New forms of production organisation within large firms – such as the network form, the modular organisation of production, and the changing nature of work whereby workers have to be more flexible and responsible – have also been identified. However, the paradigm on which policy analysis is based has remained the same, centred on exchange and on the capacity of the market to reach equilibrium on its own. In this context, industrial policy as a long-term vision is not necessary, as in the long term markets adjust and lead to optimal results if competition is as free as possible.

We do not mean that the objectives of undistorted competition and openness to exchange with the rest of the world are not pertinent, but that a change in production organisation has important social and political implications. This is true in terms of the nature of work, such as skill requirements and wages, income and standards of living, and power relations within society. An economy based on long-term employment and workers' representation in trade unions is socially and politically different from an economy where short-term flexible contracts predominate.

In a nutshell, the discussion provided in this chapter suggests that industrial development is a complex and dynamic phenomenon, with different approaches in industrial economic theory analysing different aspects. The market failure approach allows for the consideration of only limited aspects. A long-term vision is necessary, identifying possible development paths and providing levers to make some paths more likely and to mobilise society towards specific objectives, as we will discuss in greater detail in the next chapter.

CONCLUSIONS: UNBUNDLING AND THE RISING IMPORTANCE OF INTANGIBLE ASSETS

Smith describes the advantages of the modern organisation by relating the capacity to learn and therefore to accumulate knowledge within a specific activity. One example is the knowledge accumulated from repetition, which permits task optimisation and enhanced knowledge of materials and tools in the defining and designing of new instruments and machines. The capacity also exists to develop knowledge through experience and dedicated studies aimed at improving the organisation of production: dividing up work and articulating its cycle in phases and sequential tasks, and thereby reducing lead times. The required knowledge is therefore somewhat technical, related to a single task and the function of productive transformation. There is also a specific learning effect related to the capacity to design and manage a complete productive organisation. How can this organisation be defined?

In Chapter 3 of his book, Smith answers by suggesting that there is no unique and perfect model for organising production, although it must always be related to the exchange system to which it belongs or, even better, to the level and type of competition. Market knowledge complements technical and organisational knowledge. We must understand its configuration, the role of competitors and the nature of the traded goods. The union of technical, organisational and market knowledge determines the productivity improvements that are the basis of economic development.

In such a model, the capacity to create value is clearly related to the capacity to focus human competencies on the production of goods within an organisational model that accumulates and transfers technical, organisational and market knowledge into the productive cycle. The explanations provided by Smith are related to productive capacity. Through different examples he reminds us that as the scope of the market increases, it is possible to define a deeper division of labour: to further develop the capacity to incorporate knowledge and therefore to increase the value of goods offered on the market.

Specialisation and complementarity within a dynamic context are the key to efficiency, and therefore to competitiveness. The capacity to design new methods of organisation, to introduce new machines, to identify new needs and to open new markets, constitutes the essential component through which this efficiency becomes a competitive advantage. Smith called these innovations 'secrets', and claimed that although the advantages derived from such secrets permitted continuously high profits, they would attract new competitors. While trade secrets are difficult to maintain, 'secrets in manufacturing are capable of being longer kept than secrets in trade. A dyer who has found the means of producing a particular colour with materials which cost only half of the price of those commonly made use of, may, with good management, enjoy the advantage of his discovery as long as he lives, and even leave it as a legacy to his posterity' (Smith, 1776, p. 77).

Knowledge, learning and innovation are therefore sources of competitive advantage that combine together to represent the engine of social development. An economy becomes more dynamic as its knowledge base spreads and as its organisation of production is increasingly based on learning. The essence of the knowledge-based, post-crisis economy can be summarised with this metaphor. We have moved from an economy based on the work done, to an economy based on the work to be done.

We therefore think that there is an urgent need for studies of production organisation, which could empirically check which phases of the production process are offshored and which are not, and which tasks are associated. We do not pretend to provide a new explanation that is superior to previous ones. We just hope to stress a particular element of the analysis of firm structure and market competition that appears to have been rather neglected in the past and which should be a focus of attention to hopefully better understand the complexity of industrial development and derive appropriate industrial policies.

In this perspective, the long-term cannot be assumed to be characterised by automatic adjustment. Structural changes arise in long-term adjustment processes, where firms operate by trial and error, adjusting the work done to the work to be done. When the extent of the market changes, the division of labour has to be adapted. Economic development does not arise without a structural adjustment of its internal relationships, both economic and social. The implications of this analysis for the definition of industrial policies are derived in the next chapter.

This chapter has shown that production and labour organisation are key determinants of development. The globalisation process is inducing a re-organisation of production processes on a global scale, whereby the "word done" is unbundled globally but the "work to be done" is concentrated, as knowledge becomes the heart of production. While the crisis has shown that leaving the system unregulated does not function, the new industrial policy accompanying this process is not a return to subsidies or direct intervention of state in markets but a policy based on two major axes, which we will elaborate in the next chapters. The first axis is that of innovation and territory, because the system cannot grow if innovation is only internal to firms but rather the territory has to valorise skills and competencies. The second axis is that of entitlements and provisions, namely relating rights to development processes, promoting the right to participate in collective learning processes.

4. A framework for defining industrial policy

INTRODUCTION

This chapter reviews the main approaches to industrial economics and policy which lead to different recommendations on industrial policy. It shows that the theoretical framework that emerges leads to a justification of industrial policy only on the basis of the existence of 'failures'. Market failures justify public intervention in markets in the neoclassical paradigm; government failures justify the preference for no government intervention; systemic failures are what governments should address in formulating (essentially research and development and innovation) policies within evolutionary theories.

These approaches are useful to point to specific problems in the economic system, but in our view they lead to an industrial policy consisting of a series of independent actions without a broad vision. Markets and institutions build up a system where economic institutions co-evolve with social and political institutions. The point is thus to provide the right gears and levers to guide the industrial development process towards more desirable paths, making it more likely that certain directions are taken. Our framework is therefore one of political economy in the sense of Robbins (1981).

Our approach is holistic, with the idea that the properties of the industrial system cannot be explained by its component parts alone. As Aristotle put it, the whole is more than the sum of the parts.

In this perspective, the analysis of production organisation is essential. Production organisation is determined by the firm's characteristics, its internal and external environments, social and political institutions, the extent of the market, and product requirements. In turn, production organisation has implications on the social, economic and political characteristics of the economic system in which the firm is embedded. In other words, the division of labour determines the productive power of labour (productivity) that has to be defined according to the extent of the market, but it also determines working conditions and the living standards of workers, hence their access to education and to cultural development. Inventions and technical progress in turn depend on the culture and knowledge that originate from experience. It is in this respect that industrial policy has to be determined in a holistic way: industrial development is determined by, and in turn influences, the characteristics and evolution of society and its cultural development. So industrial development policies must take account not only of available resources and technologies, but also of the social characteristics of the territory and the training of human resources that simultaneously determine social and economic evolution. We represent this definition of industrial policy, in a 'sundial' framework of industrial development.

Smith stressed the importance of culture and knowledge for development, using the example of the American colonies. In such colonies, English immigrants brought their culture and knowledge which enabled the development of a rural and then urban middle class; in contrast the development of Spanish and Portuguese colonies was limited by the feudal culture and its highly segregated society.

THE STATE AND THE MARKET

The role of the state in the economy, and in industrial development in particular, appears to be justified by a number of 'failures': market, government and systemic.

Market Failures

Markets, in order to generate an optimal allocation of resources, must function in conditions of perfect competition. These conditions are rarely found in reality. For example, information is imperfect and incomplete, asymmetrically distributed between individuals. The technology of production may be such that it is more efficient for a monopoly to serve the market (a natural monopoly). Conditions in which the market does not generate the social optimum are defined (in neoclassical theory) as market failures, generally justifying state intervention.

There are four main types of market failures:

1. Externalities, whereby a third party to a transaction is affected (negatively or positively) by it; in case of negative effects (such as pollution) the state intervenes through command-and-control or incentive-based regulation.
2. Internalities, whereby failures arise within the transaction, as in the case of asymmetric information (for example, in labour or some product markets, such as medicines); generally, product or labour regulation solves these problems.
3. Public goods (defence, street lights, and so on), which are non-rival (the consumption by one individual does not reduce the quantity available to other individuals) and non-excludable (it is impossible to prevent one individual from consuming the good; for example, the light in the streets); generally the state provides such goods because no firm can find it profitable to produce them.
4. Market power, which may result naturally, as in the case of a natural monopoly, or from abuse of a dominant position or predatory actions. In the first case, the state intervenes through regulation; in the second, through antitrust policy.

In terms of industrial policy, market failures justify competition policy and regulation of network industries, of products and labour markets, as well as environmental policy. This is extremely useful, but it has two major drawbacks. First, it tends to convey a static view of industry: market failures arise once and disappear when corrected. Second, it tends to lead to a fragmentation of industrial development policies: competition policy, innovation policy, regulation, and trade policy are all treated separately, but they have an overall impact on industrial development. This does not mean that the market failure approach is not useful; however, a long-term holistic vision makes it possible to consider the whole and not just the parts, as well as the dynamics of the industrial development process.

In our view, industrial policy is about shaping industrial restructuring and development, favouring certain generic technologies that are assessed as strategic because they provide key inputs (such as energy) or because they have high potential growth, with potential applications in many sectors. The government has to intervene to sustain investment in some areas because market forces alone do not provide clear enough indications of the profitability of resources that do not actually exist, such as a new technology.

Static models which assume exogenously given factor endowments in one country relative to another are unlikely to be appropriate. When a country wishes to spur the development of new sectors in the economy, such as Germany implementing an explicit policy to develop competence in biotechnologies from the 1990s onwards (Lehrer and Asakawa, 2004), it has to act on factor endowments and cannot take them as given. Thus research and development has to be favoured in order to increase the knowledge base (the endowment in knowledge), while the education system has to be mobilised to provide appropriate skills (researchers specialised in the new technology, engineers and technicians, and so on). The market failure argument can be used to justify public intervention to increase skills (via education programmes) and research and development (private investments are generally not optimal from a social point of view). But no indication of the particular tasks that have to be favoured is given from this unless an analysis of production processes is performed. Even then, the latter analysis may be inconclusive.

An analysis of production organisation and the economic system should be performed with a long-term perspective, highlighting historical evolution and trends that make certain developments more likely. The market failure approach tends to lead to a fragmentation of industrial policies into specific actions, each aimed at specific market failures, without a broad perspective. Markets may efficiently favour the maximisation of short-term profits, so that no market failure appears. However, long-term perspectives are essential.

For instance, from the point of view of the efficiency of corporate governance, the separation of ownership and control has been shown to better ensure that firms maximise profits. A reliance on capital markets allows for the punishment of managers who do not maximise profits and act in the interest of the firm's value, although the crisis has shown that these results are not always confirmed. Therefore, from the point of view of market failure, distributed shareholding is better than concentrated shareholding. However, the reliance on capital markets has also been shown to lead firm managers to focus on short-term profits, at the expense of long-term investments. Thus some firms are led to redistribute their profits to shareholders instead of investing in costly (in the short-term) activities that may, however, yield high competitiveness in the long-term.

In addition, a firm may find it appealing to delocalise its activities away from a certain territory because this maximises its profits, but this may not favour the industrial and economic development of the territory which the firm leaves, because the firm's departure leaves many people unemployed and local suppliers in crisis. The territory's government may find that persuading the firm not to leave is a useful industrial policy, although from a market failure point of view this is not justified.

Our analysis is that the current crisis is due to the inability of the economic system, markets and institutions to adapt to the dramatic structural changes brought about by globalisation. There was not one market failure, but many market failures and, more fundamentally, a structural adjustment problem of the system that has to be addressed.

Government Failures

When bureaucrats and policymakers are considered to be self-interested individuals, government failures may arise. These failures occur when they pursue their own interests at the expense of the interests of the community, or when they are 'captured' by interest groups or lobbies of various types. In the presence of information asymmetries – which imply that the behaviour of policymakers cannot be perfectly monitored – adopted policies can be wrong from a welfare point of view.

Pushing this argument to the extreme, this implies that the best solution is to leave the market to work freely or keep intervention to a minimum. However, looking at the experience of most countries that have reached a high industrial development level, both industrialised and newly 'emerged' economies, it is very difficult to find a case where governments have not implemented some sort of industrial policy, in the sense of shaping and promoting industrial development. Even the US did this by promoting research and development in defence-related sectors and favouring 'buy American', using public procurement as a tool to develop sectors such as aviation (Bianchi and Labory, 2010).

Both market and government failures have supported the 'neo-liberal' view. Given the likely appearance of government failures, public intervention must be kept to a minimum: the minimum being pure market failures. In fact, claiming that the solution to economic problems is to leave the market to itself involves a value judgement:

namely that whatever solutions the market freely leads to is better than any attempt by the state to somehow adjust the evolution of the economic system. Losers will lose just because they are inefficient and deserve to lose, even if that means falling into poverty. Similarly, abandoning an industrial policy because firms are better able to decide on their restructuring – and in any case the state cannot pick winners – implies the same value judgement.

The unpredictability of the tasks that will be offshored and those which will remain in the country as the process of unbundling goes on may also be used as an argument against state intervention, using the same value judgement. However, economic systems are complex and their evolution highly difficult to predict. As stressed by Robbins (1981, p. 3), 'quantitative prediction in economics is apt to be hazardous'. Economics is not a natural science where a theory's validity depends on its ability to predict economic outcome. If this were the case, the last financial crisis would have been avoided.

We further argue that any policy recommendations necessarily involve value judgement. Robbins (1981) pointed to the desirability of returning to a political economy perspective in the sense that economics cannot be a science and necessarily implies value judgements. 'There might be utility in the broad sense in the working of the institutions of well-run slave state, and yet the assumptions behind my Political Economy would reject them' (1981, p. 8).

As we will argue in what follows, the consideration of entitlements and provisions allows for the definition of industrial policy in a political economy framework, because they take account of rights and human freedom.

Systemic Failures

The evolutionary theory has outlined the importance of a third type of failure, namely systemic failure. When technical progress is determined in 'systems of innovation' – whereby all actors of the innovative process are interrelated and the density and effectiveness of the relationships is key to determining the extent of innovation and its commercial success – it is clear that failures of systems or networks have to be corrected in order to increase innovation. Von Tunzelmann (2010) has analysed technology policy in post-war Britain, arguing that network failures have created more problems than market failures although policy was more officially justified by the latter failures. According to the author, technology policy must be designed taking into account the system innovation processes of which they are a part. Thus instruments aimed at increasing the innovative effort will be effective only if the overall system is coherent. Von Tunzelmann provides the example of the Lisbon Strategy, which sows systemic failures within it given that budget constraints on the macro side suggest countries should follow restrictive economic policies, while technological imperatives would dictate expansive economic policies.

This analysis of systemic failures can be extended to the whole economic system, and not confined to technological development. It is therefore very interesting since it recognises the economic system as complex and dynamic, and suggests governing systemic failures in order to guide the system towards appropriate development paths.

New comparative advantages (be they defined at sector or task level) and new industries develop in territories where the presence of a system allows synergies between various actors to be realised. For instance, spin-off firms are created from the interaction between a scientist, who makes a discovery with potential product application, and an entrepreneur, who brings management and business competencies. There might be systemic failures in industrial systems that prevent the restructuring of old industries and the birth of new ones.

According to Von Tunzelmann, and as shown by his example of the Lisbon Strategy, systemic failures also include problems raised by the lack of coherence between different policies. Industrial policy will be ineffective if macroeconomic or trade policies are incoherent. Von Tunzelmann provides another example of systemic failure raised by incoherence. He argues that the corporate governance regime prevailing in the UK has also created problems for innovation and acted as an obstacle to the effectiveness of innovation policies. The market-led system of the UK has led to short-termism in management and the impossibility of adopting long-term strategic decisions such as investment in technological development. Short-termism is due to the pressure of powerful capital interests and pressures to increase dividends for shareholders. The market for corporate control worked all too well, favouring aggressive takeovers that impeded firms from adopting strategic long-term visions.

Von Tunzelman argues that there is a need for a better alignment of actor interests and objectives in the innovation system, at all levels: micro, meso and macro. Networking policies are important in order to ensure better alignment. This is true for technological development, but also for industrial development in general. For instance, old industries are more able to adapt to changing competitive conditions if the system is effective in bringing about interactions with agents that can suggest solutions to the problems of old industries, or suggest the application of new technologies that can upgrade existing products or even change those products.

This approach, although limited to the sphere of technological progress, is useful and very similar to our approach aiming to identify the gears and levers of industrial development to bring the economic system into desirable paths.

PROVISIONS AND ENTITLEMENTS AS KEY ELEMENTS OF ECONOMIC DEVELOPMENT

Two important elements of industrial development are resources and rules. Resources include knowledge and human capital, as well as raw materials and infrastructures. Rules are both social (in some societies some categories of people are excluded from economic activities, such as some castes in India, or women in Islamic societies) and institutional (laws and regulations that determine, for instance, access to education or the procedures to create firms). Countries have different sets of rules and resources that determine different production organisation capacities and hence different paths in industrial development. Rules and resources are not fixed through time. On the contrary, they constantly evolve as a result of demographic, cultural and political trends.

In turn, rules and resources determine the capacity of the economic system to organise production, in the sense that they determine feasible technologies, feasible contracts with employees, available raw materials, and available skills. Rules and resources therefore appear as levers which industrial policymakers can activate in order to favour industrial development.

The concepts of resources and rules can be made more precise by referring to Dahrendorf's analysis in *The Modern Social Conflict. An Essay on the Politics of Liberty* (1988), which he revised in 2008.[1] Dahrendorf defines the concepts of provisions and entitlements in a way that is similar to but more precise than our concepts of resources and rules. Entitlements refer to socially defined means of access;

essentially to goods, but not only goods. Sen (1982) defined entitlements, referring only to goods. Dahrendorf extends the concept to include non-economic commodities such as the right to vote and the right to be educated: there are civil rights (basic elements of the rule of law and equality before the law), social rights (the universal right to real income) and political rights (suffrage, freedom of association and freedom of speech). Entitlements open up choices in our commodity purchase, in our use of the education system, and in our voice in the political system. The set of choices (in the sense of objects from which to choose, not of the act of choosing) opened up by entitlements is what Dahrendorf calls 'provisions'.

Both entitlements and provisions are key determinants of the development of nations: of their growth from not only an economic, but also a social, political and cultural point of view (what we shall call, in Smithian terms, the wealth of nations). Thus Dahrendorf gives the examples of the industrial revolution and the French revolution of the eighteenth century. While the former was essentially a revolution of provisions, leading to an enormous growth in provisions, the latter was essentially a revolution of entitlements, concerned with enlarging human rights and the rights of citizens. Both provisions and entitlements are necessary for economic development, or more generally the wealth of nations. Thus capitalism, and the enormous increase in provisions it has brought, would not have developed without the prior development of entitlements throughout the eighteenth and nineteenth centuries.

A more recent example is that of developing countries. The policies recommended by the International Monetary Fund (IMF) or the World Bank to developing countries have concerned provisions and not entitlements, often increasing the wealth of the already rich in these countries and leaving the poor in the same situation as before since their entitlements, such as access to education, jobs and goods, did not change. As Dahrendorf puts it (2008, p. 15): 'Unless traditional entitlement structures are broken and elements of civil society created, macroeconomic growth means little for the many, however satisfactory the International Monetary Fund may find the statistics'.

In fact, Dahrendorf argues that economics has become a science of provisions, while politics and sociology have specialised in entitlements. The problem is that the two are interrelated and must be taken simultaneously into account. Economic progress presupposes both, and for Dahrendorf taking both elements into account means

```
          Provisions

          ┌─────────────┬─────────────┐
          │             │    ▶ (B)    │
          │    – +      │    + +      │
          │             │  (A)  (C)   │
          │             │      ↑      │
          │             ↗      │      │
          │             │             │
          │    – –      │    + –      │
          │             │             │
          └─────────────┴─────────────┘
                                         Entitlements
```

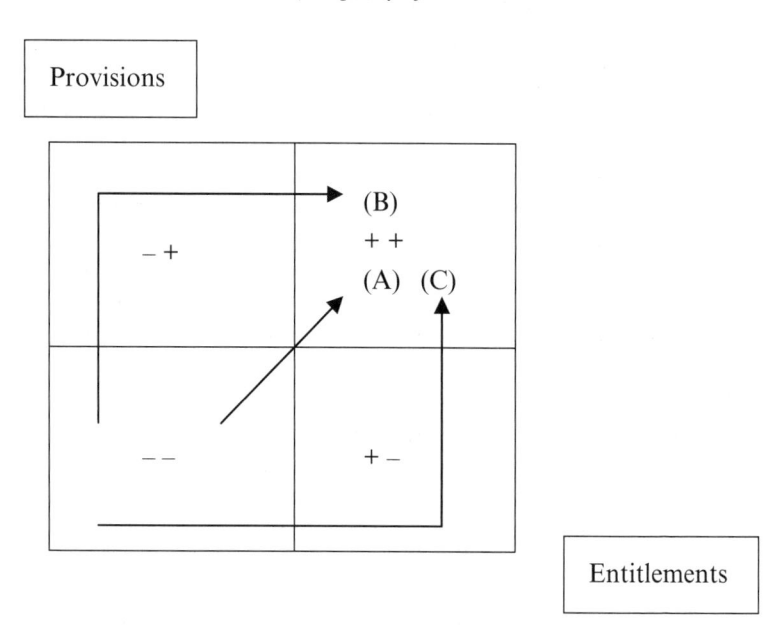

Figure 4.1   The relationship between provisions and entitlements

building a civil society. The interrelation of provisions and entitlements, of economics and politics, is shown in the fact that civil rights provide access to markets and therefore help their extension, while rising income is a necessary precondition for an entitlement to a decent standard of living.

Countries have different trajectories of industrial development according to their sets of provisions and entitlements. Some countries have levels of provisions and entitlements that are quite balanced and lead to a balanced path of industrial development (path A in Figure 4.1). This is the path chosen by the EU in the economic integration process (see Chapter 6). Some have high levels of provisions but low levels of entitlements (path B), which is the case of China. Others, such as South Africa, have low levels of provisions but high levels of entitlements (path C).[2]

Provisions and entitlements determine the capacity to organise production, hence simultaneously the efficiency and equity of a system. For instance, the division of labour characterising the British industrial revolution was made possible by the transformation of the feudal society into a bourgeois society, and in turn had implications on the development of a working class, leading to less poverty and more education within the population. Experiments with the division of labour in British firms at that time implied a significant increase in productivity (efficiency) but also in equity (poverty was reduced, although the living conditions of workers at that time was still quite hard). In turn, that industrial development fed increases in equity and efficiency (more access to education and the resulting higher capacity of workers who could contribute to higher productivity and efficiency).

In this framework, industrial policy has a clear role. By acting on provisions and entitlements the government influences industrial development and consequently both 'justice and happiness', in the sense of equity (the capacity of all individuals to take part in economic activities) and standards of living (the type of work one has access to determines income, skills, capacity to learn, access to leisure and culture).

We can also relate this framework to the discussion of industrial policy in the current post-crisis context we have carried out so far. What globalisation has essentially meant is a rise in the diversity of players in world exchange, and hence in the complexity of industrial development. New players have emerged, with different cultural and social characteristics, basing their development on particular provisions and entitlements.

Whereas before the 1990s world trade was dominated by trade between developed countries, with similar provisions and entitlements (culture, labour, regulation and so on), nowadays world trade is characterised by intense competition where the old players (the developed countries of the Western world, such as the US, Europe and Japan) have progressively lost market share to new players, such as China and India. These countries are characterised by specific provisions and entitlements.

For instance, China has abundant cheap and relatively skilled labour, together with limited entitlements (rights) that include extreme working conditions, little care for the environment and no freedom of speech (path B in Figure 4.1). These provisions and entitlements have led to exponential growth, but at the cost of human rights and environmental protection. Chinese products flow to the rest of the world because they are cheap. This raises a deep industrial policy problem for Western countries: should they adjust their provisions and entitlements to Chinese standards to reach a similar industrial development path, or should China be made to raise its level of entitlements so that equity in China gets closer to the equity levels of the Western world?

Dahrendorf (2008) seems to suggest that China should be made to raise its levels of entitlements because only by doing so can it become a civil society. An interesting point that Dahrendorf stresses here is that a single country can no longer develop its civil society on its own, but depends on other countries in the world making similar progress due to the high level of interactions between them.

In the post-war world, Western countries dominated by the US dictated the levels of entitlements necessary for development. International organisations, such as the United Nations (UN), aimed at consolidating the importance of democracy and human rights and diffusing them to developing countries. The 'multilateral' world of today, where Western countries and values no longer dominate, has to define new entitlements. New challenges have also emerged, such as environmental protection, which is essentially an entitlement problem (the right of access to a clean environment). However, the new players in world trade do not seem to be willing to accept such constraints. This was shown by the failure of international discussions about climate change policies in Kyoto in 1998; developing countries are not ready to pay the cost of environmental damage until they reach certain levels of development.

Globalisation has brought about a change in the way access to fundamental rights is provided. Rights used to be guaranteed through long-term contracts, providing secure jobs for life. Through contributions, social assistance and access to health services and pensions in old age were also guaranteed. The changing production organisation examined in Chapter 2 has forced governments to change labour legislation and new forms of contracts have been made possible. Many workers have now short-term or other forms of flexible contracts, which no longer guarantee access to social assistance, health services or pensions. The state has also lost control over labour relations as a result of delocalisation and the transformation of large, integrated firms where trade unions used to bargain over labour contracts. This does not necessarily mean that workers' rights have been reduced but that they need to be reformulated. Fundamental labour rights that affect individual workers are identity, income and security. These rights are also fundamental to shaping life and personality.

The organisation of production today is characterised by a division of labour often organised on a global scale, exploiting complementarities between different parts of the world. Phases of the production process are spread across different countries, according to the level of resources and capabilities available. In such a context, complementarities arise between countries, and the world system of production becomes very complex. Industrial development no longer depends on one country only but on various ones. The definition of entitlements, representing one lever of industrial development, can no longer be decided individually by a country but only by all (or a group of) countries, in a coordinated manner.

It is in this sense that the European experience is illuminating. As argued in Chapter 6, European economic integration means that industrial development becomes a matter not only of single countries but also (and foremost) of the whole, of the EU. The primary industrial policy of the EU is therefore the economic integration process itself, because it requires the definition of a common vision of economic and industrial development, with common objectives which, in the EU, are laid down in its treaties (harmonious economic development that respects the environment; high levels of employment and social protection; constantly improving conditions and quality of life; and economic and social cohesion within and between countries). The economic integration process has thus led to the coordinated development of both provisions and entitlements in the EU and has resulted in European countries embarking on a similar path of development (path A in Figure 4.1).

Path C in Figure 4.1 characterises a country such as South Africa, where entitlements, namely civil rights, have only recently been extended to the whole population, and the economic opportunities for the black population remain low due to a lack of provisions (see Chapter 5).

In the market failure approach, industrial policy does not really make sense because it does not have instruments of its own. There are no ministries or agencies in charge of industrial policy for this reason (Välilä, 2006). Industrial policy is implemented through fiscal policy (subsidies, grants and tax exemptions), trade policy (access to foreign markets and access of foreign firms to the domestic market), competition policy, social policy (such as education, life-long training and workers' protection) and even macroeconomic policy (influencing inflation, exchange rates and interest rates).

It is true that industrial development is determined by many factors, not only those related to industry characteristics but also macroeconomic, labour and other policies. For this reason, industrial policy has to be considered as a vision, a strategy of industrial development in a political economy framework. Industrial development, and more generally economic growth, arise when the whole economy is appropriately geared to it. However, we disagree with the conclusions of Välilä that industrial policy cannot be considered and thought about. Industrial policy is about complex interactions within the economy and no simple solution exists to spur industrial development. However, a broad vision coming out of broad reflection is necessary for all its components to be coherent and complementary.

As we will show in the last chapter, this is precisely what the European Commission seemed to suggest at the beginning of the twenty-first century, by proposing a strategy for economic growth to which all member states would adhere and by underlining the importance of an integrated vision of industrial development. In this view industrial policy is considered in a broad sense not only to correct market failures but also to favour structural change, review crisis industries and develop new industries including, but not limited to, those that are science-based.

INDUSTRIAL POLICY AS A VISION OF INDUSTRIAL DEVELOPMENT

The consideration of industrial policy as a vision of industrial development implies the explicit analysis of the complementarities between instruments and between implementation levels. Defining such an industrial policy allows all policy fields and all levels to share the same objective of industrial development (and development in a broad, classic sense).

Once this view is adopted, two issues arise. First, the design of industrial policy requires the identification of industry's current and future expected trends, of crisis industries and of the technologies of the future and the possible applications of such technologies. This analysis should allow for the identification of possible scenarios of future industrial development which policymakers have to choose between. The choice of the industrial development path to favour is both very risky (for example, choosing a technology that is rapidly surpassed by a new one) and very costly (resources are required to identify scenarios and above all to invest in the new technologies). However, the potential gain for the country as a whole, in terms of industrial and civil development, wealth of nations, is very high.

Industrial policy choice is also very political. Stakeholders have to be involved in order for the vision to be shared and approved. In dictatorial regimes, such as Italy in the 1930s, industrial policy choices are imposed. In democracies, consultation with all interested parties is necessary in order to increase the probability of success, both because consulting interested parties allows policymakers to better access relevant information and so make better-informed and more appropriate choices, and also because consensus indicates that implementation will be more closely followed. The need for consensus on economic policy confirms there are implied value judgements on which all stakeholders have to agree.

Industrial policy choices must also be made holistically, considering the interdependencies between instruments and policy levels, between strategy and organisations, organisations and their environment, and so on. The economic system is complex and industrial development is determined by complex interdependencies and processes. Industrial policy as a long-term vision of industrial development implies the abandonment of methodological individualism by considering the specific industrial development problem within the overall system of which it is a part. Just as individual actions within societies are largely explained by the characteristics of the whole society, especially its social norms and culture, firms' strategies and organisation are determined by the characteristics of the economic system of which they are a part: the institutions, the extent of the market and the characteristics of other related markets.

Industrial policy as a long-term vision of industrial development, leading to and backed by a civil society, can therefore be represented as shown in Figure 4.2.

A Framework for Industrial Policy as a Long-term Vision

Entitlements and provisions are essential elements of industrial policy. Using our reflection on industrial policy in the twenty-first century (Bianchi and Labory, 2006a, b; 2009), we identify two other dimensions or levels of development, namely innovation and

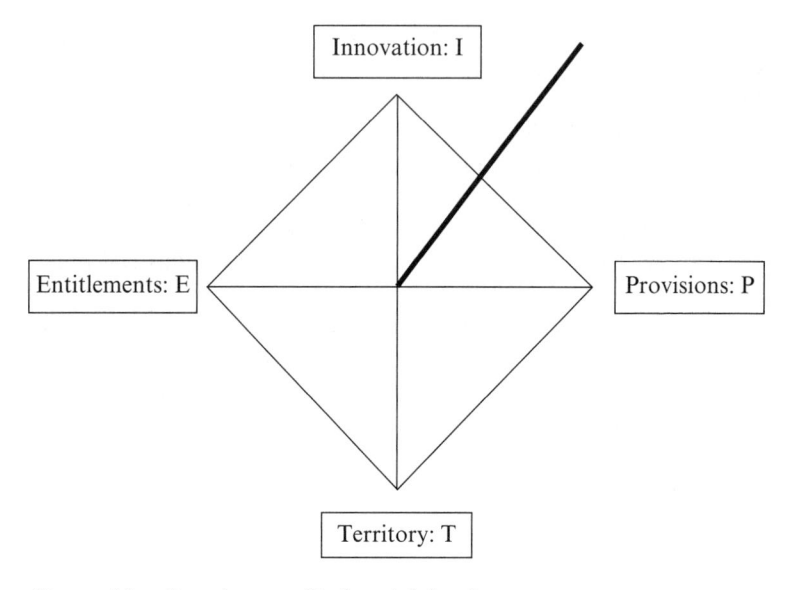

```
        ┌──────────────┐
        │ Innovation: I│
        └──────────────┘
              ◇
┌────────────┐   ┌────────────┐
│Entitlements:E│◀─┼─▶│Provisions: P│
└────────────┘   └────────────┘
              ◇
        ┌──────────────┐
        │ Territory: T │
        └──────────────┘
```

Figure 4.2 Four levers of industrial development

territory. Entitlements determine the rights of individuals to take part in development as well as in productive and competitive processes. Provisions determine their knowledge, competencies and resources, and hence their capability to take part in these processes, together with other resources necessary to perform economic activities. Innovation is the capacity to create knowledge and to apply this new knowledge to production processes; it is a dynamic element that sustains development. The territory dimension highlights the importance of the embeddedness of productive processes in territories, where they can gain from local resources such as social capital and infrastructure (Figure 4.2).

All these levers are important and are not substitutes for each other. Sustainable industrial policy should aim at using all four levers, coherently defining and implementing measures at the different levels of regional, national and supranational government. These levels of government are represented by the bold line in Figure 4.2, creating a sundial.

All four elements determine both the cumulativeness and the sustainability of industrial development: cumulativeness in the sense of providing a dynamic process; sustainability essentially in the sense

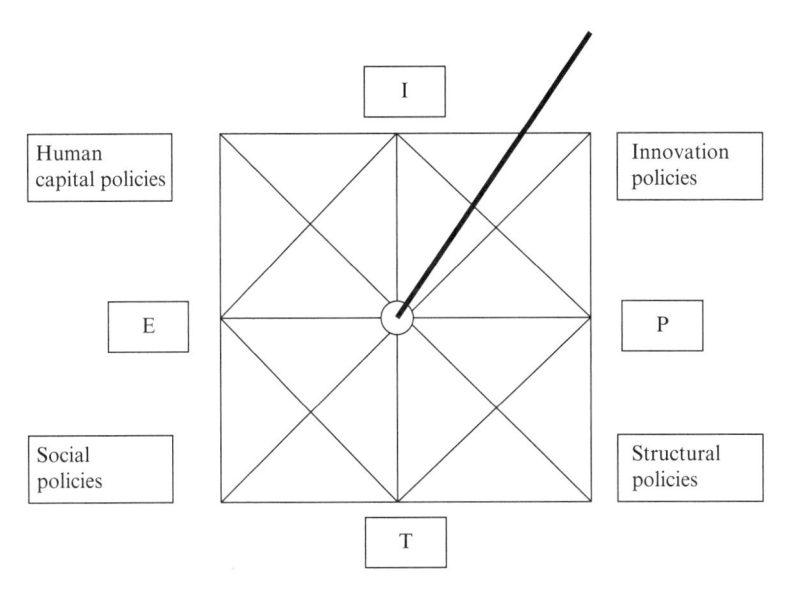

Figure 4.3 The sundial of industrial policy: the EPIT framework

of the compatibility of the economic, social and political spheres. These dimensions are not substitutes but complementary, and have to be simultaneously developed in order for industrial development to be sustainable from both social and environmental points of view.

In fact, the four levers can enable a virtuous circle of development: innovation spurs regional development and social improvements, which in turn enlarge entitlements, allowing more people to take part in the development process, which enables further innovation. The model is therefore essentially dynamic, not representing the development process itself but both the elements to take into account in the policy decision-making process as well as their links. These elements and their links indeed determine possible learning mechanisms.

The model of entitlements, provisions, innovation and territory sets up all possible public policies, as shown in Figure 4.3.

The overall area defined by the four elements can be divided along the different axes drawn, thereby determining areas that show different focuses of policies. The IOP area is that of traditional industrial policies, consisting of measures to develop resources, such as infrastructure and financing for firms, and measures to promote innovation. The IOT area is that of social policies, since people are primarily part of territorial communities and their social well-being is intimately linked to it. New social policies also include the provision of learning capacity to workers and therefore extend to the whole IET area. Entitlements are another key element of not only social policies, but also human capital policies in the sense of training and education. Providing the population with the relevant skills is indeed essential to industrial and economic development. The ETP area is that of urban and environmental policies.

If the dial leans towards the provisions pole, away from entitlements, the risk is reaching what can be called a 'Chinese syndrome', where there is growth of provisions without entitlements. This growth is unsustainable from a social point of view because economic growth is not supported by redistributive and participative justice. In contrast, if the dial is shifted towards entitlements, without simultaneously developing provisions, we have high social demands that cannot possibly be fulfilled, given the lack of resources. If the dial is pushed too far towards innovation, the risk is of non-embedded change, while pushing excessively towards territory risks leading to conservation without the ability to manage change.

CONCLUSION

The sundial therefore expresses the need for coherence between the different levers. It is not necessary that all countries be perfectly in equilibrium, but if the sundial leans towards one pole or another it can indicate policy adjustments are needed and suggest possible actions for policymakers so that their long-term vision and implementation become more coherent and effective. These are industrial policies after the crisis: the capacity to view in the long-term the complexity of society and to define policies that could guarantee their economic, social and human development.

The axes on the dial can also change over time as new priorities emerge. For instance, the terms implicit in the EU Lisbon Strategy (Chapter 6) may be better termed as knowledge instead of innovation (because of its emphasis on the knowledge-based economy where not only innovation, or knowledge creation, is essential but also the transfer and accumulation of existing knowledge); and environment (particularly environmental concerns) instead of territory. Instead of entitlements, related to the right of access to collective goods, there is the concept of capabilities, defined by Amartya Sen as not only access rights but also the capacity and the competency necessary to execute these rights. Provisions become human capital, which is key to activate all three of the other elements.

Development depends both on the extension of the base of the four elements (knowledge, environment, capabilities and human capital) and on the coherence between the instruments that the state, at regional, national and supranational level), implements in order to develop and coordinate the four key elements. The sundial therefore represents a holistic approach to industrial policy, trying to understand the mechanics of the whole in which industry is a component part in order to favour sustainable development, namely industrial development that is compatible with social development, equity and environmental preservation for future generations.

The next two chapters illustrate this framework with concrete examples.

NOTES

1. *The Modern Social Conflict. The Politics of Liberty*, completely revised second edition (Dahrendorf, 2008).
2. These cases are illustrated in Chapter 5.

5. Industrial policies as long-term strategies: some examples

INTRODUCTION

In this chapter, we wish to illustrate our industrial policy framework using a few examples. These examples show the necessary coherence between the main pillars of the sundial we drew in the last chapter, but are not used to identify a single optimal path. In fact, it is important to stress that there is no single path to long-term, sustainable industrial development but a number of different possible routes from which a preferred one can be chosen. We suggest that this choice can be helped by the sundial which shows the requirement for coherence if development is to be sustainable and contribute to civil as well as economic development.

The sundial has four axes – entitlements, provisions, innovation and territory – that are not substitutes but complementary in contributing to industrial development. Authorities at all levels can choose to favour one or more axes, but sustainability in the competitive context of the twenty-first century requires that all axes be considered in one way or the other. The vertical fifth axis represents the coherence of industrial development policy. This is twofold: first, coherence between the different actions in the different fields, namely macro and micro, and social and economic, must be ensured; second, coherence between the levels of implementation, namely regional, national and supra-national must also be ensured.

This is a holistic approach to industrial policy, whereby the policymaker takes a broad view, trying to represent the whole system in which the particular policy issue is part, in order to identify and activate the appropriate levers for industrial development.

We illustrate this view using a number of country case studies. Each case study provides a summary of what we think are the main features of that country and the main elements of the industrial development path and industrial policy adopted (based on a literature

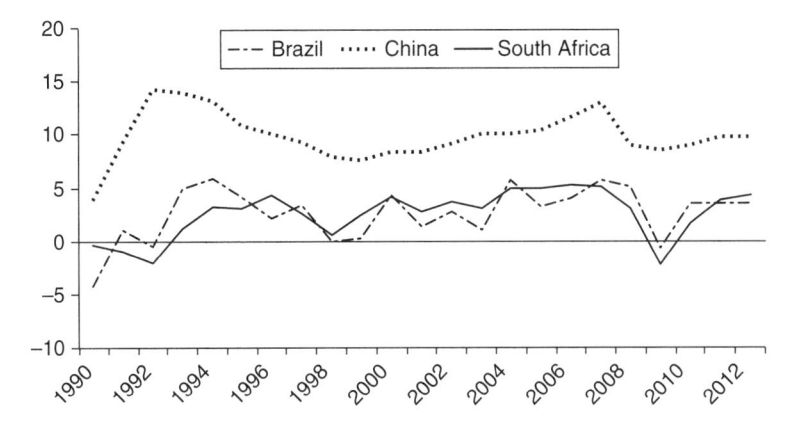

Figure 5.1 Real GDP growth in Brazil, China and South Africa, 1990 to 2012

Source: IMF data mapper, www.imf.org (most recent two years are estimates).

review and/or own experience in these countries). Inevitably we have had to perform a very broad synthesis.

We start with China and Brazil. The growth of emerging countries has been the most important aspect of the new century as already emphasised in this book. Since the 1990s, these countries have fuelled the growth of the world economy. In China, we focus on a particular region, Guangdong and the area of Shenzhen within it. The third country we mention is South Africa, because it is an interesting example where there was a lack of entitlements for a long time, followed by a sudden extension of rights that continues to create tensions because of the lack of equal distribution of provisions.

The other two countries examined are two small European countries, Ireland and Finland. We choose them because of their parallel high growth rates in the 1990s which were supported by very different approaches to industrial policy. As a result, these two countries have been very differently affected by the crisis. Given their small size, regional coherence may be less of a problem, although both countries have been concerned by this aspect too. To start with, Figures 5.1 and 5.2 illustrate the growth rates of these five countries over the period 1990 to 2012.

China is the highest growth country, sustaining high growth rates

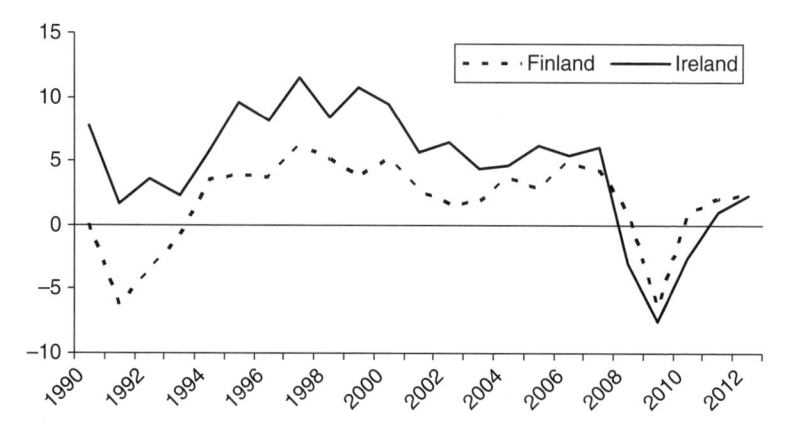

Source: IMF data mapper, www.imf.org (most recent two years are estimates).

Figure 5.2   Real GDP growth in Finland and Ireland, 1990 to 2012

throughout the period, even during the financial crisis. Brazil and South Africa have more uneven paths, while Finland and Ireland really take off in the middle of the 1990s. The latter two countries are also the hardest hit by the financial crisis, while the former three countries rapidly return to pre-crisis growth levels.

CHINA

In order to illustrate our framework we focus on a particular Chinese region, and specifically the city of Shenzhen. Shenzhen is the city which has grown most rapidly in China in the last 30 years. In 1978, Shenzhen was a fishing village, closed behind the frontier that separated the Chinese People's Republic and the booming British colony of Hong Kong.

The Shenzhen district then had 20 000 inhabitants and formed the southern part of Guangdong province, on the delta of the Pearl River. The provincial capital Guangzhou, Canton, had been the western entry port into the Chinese empire in the eighteenth century, characterised by corruption and political dependence. Adam Smith, even mentions the deprivation of the area in the *Wealth of Nations*. However, during the Mao era Guangdong became the most rapidly industrialising area of the People's Republic, based on heavy industry.

At the end of the 1970s China started the policy of setting up economic zones, and the first of these zones was created in Shenzhen in 1980. Economic zones are special areas where specific rules are implemented in order to support high growth rates. The main objectives are to attract foreign capital and to favour the creation of manufacturing activities, not only thanks to low cost labour but also to special normative and fiscal conditions in the zones that make their products internationally competitive. The economic zones can thus manufacture products that are exported to the rest of the world, on the basis of a sort of social dumping that can only be temporary.

Shenzhen was chosen by Deng Xiao Ping as the first economic zone with the idea that it could provide the productive base for Hong Kong island, thanks to its geographical location. Since then the Shenzhen economic zone has grown very rapidly, reaching 13.5 million inhabitants and attracting investment amounting to about US$ 30 billion. The Shenzhen Stock Exchange has operated since 1990 and illustrates the strong development of the financial sector in the city and region.

From an urban point of view the city expanded in two directions: one towards Canton, with the development of satellite cities integrated by a railway and metro network, and the other towards Hong Kong. The integration process has been so strong that a unique metropolitan context has been in place since 2007 which would constitute the third largest metropolitan area in the world, after New York and Tokyo.

From an economic point of view the development of Shenzhen has been supported by a strong concentration of high-tech investment, in particular by multinationals in the electronics sector, together with commercial activities in the port which are integrated with those of Canton and Hong Kong.

Extremely high growth has generated numerous problems, despite and because of so-called *hukou*, the regulations that require internal work and residence permits and limit the residence period within the economic zone. It is estimated that about 70 per cent of the Chinese workers employed in the zone do not hold *hukou*, so they have to go back to the countryside when they have finished their work contract. Parallel cities for temporary workers are also developing.

Thus a complex urban development experienced two crucial periods. In the first period a special economic zone was defined and saw the first housing developments centred on the growth of industrial areas with rather precarious residential areas alongside. In the second period it became necessary to structure the city, using urban interventions to articulate service and residential areas as the economic zone became more and more high-tech. In particular, new universities were created, including Shenzhen University, Shenzhen Polytechnic, Shenzhen Graduate School of Beijing, University, Shenzhen Institute of Information Technology and the Southern University of Science and Technology.

The rapid growth of the urban area inevitably created social problems, in particular crime. Another important type of problem created has centred on the environment. Such rapid and extensive growth has created many pollution problems, of the air water and soil.

The Shenzhen government decided to tackle the social and environmental problems by designing a long-term strategy of industrial development. International experts and business representatives, including representatives of foreign multinationals, were invited to identify the long-term development issues of the area and suggest solutions.[1] The process led to the identification of three critical issues:

1. the need to increase the quality of production and the required adjustments in education and research; hence the relationship between industrial, technological and educational dynamics;
2. the definition of environmental priorities and the redefinition of urban areas in order to address pollution and modernisation problems;
3. the need to address social problems and to extend entitlements, in particular freedom of expression, pushed by the media in Hong Kong which is still relatively free.

The case of Shenzhen shows how the issues of industrial policy, urban policy and technological policy are interrelated. It also shows the infinite set of actions that can be implemented at the different levels of policy, from town to province, region and nations, the coherence of which can only be guaranteed by defining a strategy for long-term industrial development.

A third lesson to draw from this case is that a long-term vision of industrial development can only be sustainable if entitlements are developed together with provisions. The whole of China is trying to

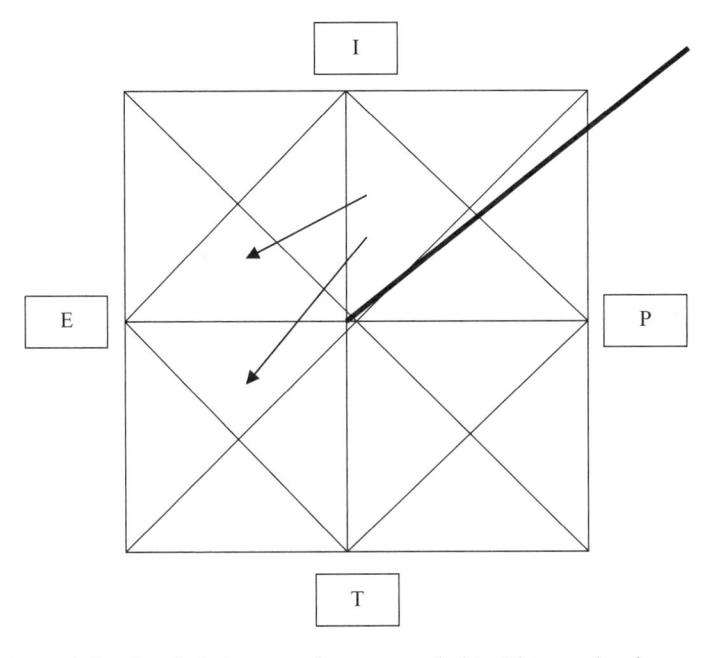

Figure 5.3 Sundial showing changes needed in Chinese development

sustain development on the basis of a growth in provisions, without due regard for entitlements such as the civil and political rights of citizens. Political élites of the communist party take all decisions at all decision-making levels. This form of development, exclusively based on provisions without entitlements, has a high cost: the need to maintain high growth rates to avoid social unrest.

China's growth obligations have pushed the government to maintain its 'dangerous liaison' with the US, buying the US deficit both to avoid an appreciation of the Yuan and to allow Americans to continue buying Chinese products. China after the crisis will be a more technological, dynamic and educated country, but also a country with higher internal inequalities and resulting instabilities. Despite this the country will have to show more responsibility and participation in global economic and political coordination now it is one of the world's biggest powers. This extreme contradiction will have to be resolved at some point.

In terms of our sundial, Chinese development can be represented by the starting point of the arrows in Figure 5.3. The direction of the arrows to the left and bottom changes in development needed to become more sustainable.

BRAZIL

Brazil is today part of the so-called BRICs countries (Brazil, Russia, India and China), which inverted the dynamics of the world economy at the beginning of the twenty-first century. By 2009 Brazil had become the world's eighth largest economy in terms of GDP, and ninth in terms of purchasing power parity (World Bank).

After a long history of colonisation, followed by political instability and dictatorship after independence, Brazil has had a democratic government since 1985. President Cardoso governed the country between 1994 and 2002 and ensured a return to economic stability. President Lula da Silva has been governing the country since 2002, implementing an interestingly balanced strategy of industrial development.

The Lula government courageously increased public spending and the poorest families' income by raising the minimum wage and pensions. This created a significant rise in internal demand both from households and from the state. Investments also increased so that overall the economy experienced a boom.

Without going into details in this short overview, Brazil provides an example of balanced industrial development in the sense that both effective rights (entitlements) and provisions have risen simultaneously. In addition, entitlements and provisions have contributed to development in a complementary way, so that development is robust and sustainable in the long-term. This synergetic development of entitlements and provisions not only boosts social cohesion but also regional cohesion, which has been a concern of the Lula government from the start.

Regional cohesion rests on developing the north-eastern states to eliminate the historical social injustice of the country and also to generate a new level of economic development that could benefit the whole country. This strategy however requires a long-term vision where investment in large infrastructures, such as the Porto Suape, is viewed not only as a development lever to generate growth around the port but also as the basis for developing trade with the rest of the world, turning these regions into worldwide exchange hubs.

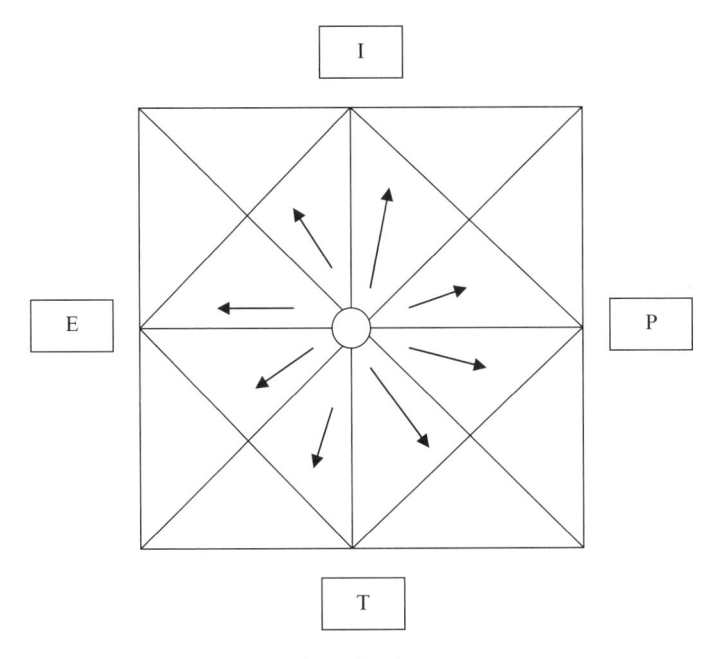

Figure 5.4 Sundial of Brazilian development

The Brazil of Lula seems to represent an attempt to simultaneously develop rights and resources, ensuring cohesion between economic development and democracy (Figure 5.4).

SOUTH AFRICA

The new South Africa started in 1994, with the end of apartheid and a change in the constitution. The history of the country started with the arrival of Dutch colonists in 1652. Their objective was not to create provinces of their home country abroad, but to create new independent states. Fighting against local populations, the Dutch colonists (Boers) expanded along the coastal area around Cape Town and the Natal Province.

When Great Britain attempted to put these areas under British dominance, lured by the discovery of diamonds and then gold, the Boers were pushed further inland, crossing the Vaal river where they founded the Transvaal and Orange Free State.

Provisions

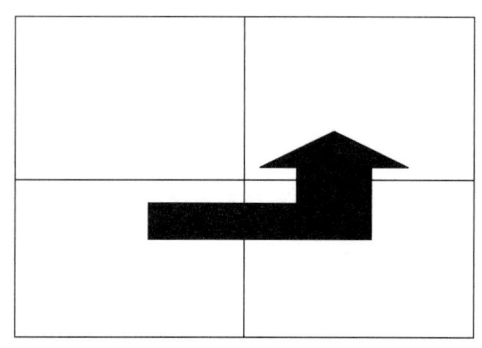

Figure 5.5 Provisions and entitlements in South Africa

Entitlements

After a new war with the British, these states were conquered and the Union of South Africa was created, gaining independence in 1910 and taking the name of the Republic of South Africa. Segregation became institutionalised and the government established three classes of race: white, coloured and black.

The republic was a state of the white, reaching standards of living comparable to the West. Coloured people were discriminated against but involved within democratic life, while blacks were left as a class without rights. After World War Two, foreign governments started to boycott South African products in protest against apartheid. Within the country, the black population started to organise and movements against apartheid expanded, of which Nelson Mandela, incarcerated for 27 years, remained a reference and leader.

At the beginning of the 1990s, in the extraordinary period of history where the Berlin Wall and bipolarity ended, apartheid also came to an end. The government took the first step towards this end in 1990 by lifting the ban on the African National Congress and other political organisations. Nelson Mandela was freed and soon became head of state. Civil and political rights were recognised for the whole population, but the economy remained in the hands of whites.

Today South Africa remains imbalanced as entitlements have been provided to the whole population but provisions are still unequally distributed, raising discontent among poorer sections of society.

Here the problems are essentially social and show that entitlements cannot be extended if provisions are not.

IRELAND

Ireland developed rapidly from the 1990s up to 2005. However, it experienced a collapse with the financial crisis, resulting from structural weaknesses that were not addressed by industrial policies. In 2008, growth fell substantially, and the public deficit rose to one of the highest levels in eurozone; prospects for living standards have gone down, while unemployment is growing.

Yet during the period 1990 to 2005 Ireland experienced average annual growth rates of more than 7 per cent, bringing commentators to speak of the 'Celtic Tiger'. The rapid fall in real GDP growth in 2008 (see Figure 5.2) led to talk about the collapse of the Irish economy, although this assessment may be somewhat exaggerated and it may be more appropriate to refer to a deep recession.

However, a number of scholars have highlighted weaknesses in the Irish economy that might have increased the sharpness of the recession and the vulnerability of the Irish industrial development path. For instance, Kirby (2010) makes a pessimistic analysis of the Irish economy. He outlines three major structural weaknesses that bring into question both the recovery of the economy after the recession and longer-term growth. First, Irish industrial development has been spurred by the growth of high-tech sectors, especially electronics and pharmaceuticals, but the bulk of the sector is foreign-owned with very few indigenous firms. Thus in 2006, output from firms assisted by Ireland's industrial development agencies included €50.6 billion from foreign-owned firms and €9.7 billion from indigenous firms, while employment was almost equally divided between the two types of firms (153 510 in foreign-owned ones and 151 610 in indigenous firms) (Kirby, 2010, pp. 6–7). The Irish high-tech sector is therefore highly dependent on foreign-owned firms, mainly US ones.

Irish industrial policy has essentially focused on attracting foreign direct investment (FDI) using a number of measures including maintaining low tax rates (Bailey et al., 2010). The development of indigenous firms has only recently represented a concern. Only in 1994 did a programme for small businesses start in Ireland, with the 'Small Business Operational Programme'. The indigenous firm sector is not only small, it is also not innovative with low investment in research and development, and low product and process innovation. The focus on FDI attraction not only led to maintaining low tax rates but also to adopting other types of measures to ensure the competitiveness of the Irish economy. One such measure has been social partnership agreements on moderate wage increases in return for lower tax rates.[2] Such agreements have been adopted since 1987 (Bailey et al., 2010a), with six such social pacts adopted between 1988 and 2005. Ireland also chose to favour FDI in particular sectors, namely electronics and pharmaceuticals, chosen because of their high growth prospects and low transport costs. Another measure to attract this investment has been the training of skilled labour able to work in these particular sectors.

The second weakness according to Kirby is social failure, or what we could call a lack of coherence between economic growth and social cohesion. The Irish boom disproportionately benefited technical professionals and self-employed small business entrepreneurs. They gained high incomes while a substantial part of the population remained on low-incomes or even in poverty. Relative poverty in fact increased during the years of the Irish boom: the percentage of the population with income at 50 per cent or less of the average rose from 18.6 per cent in 1994 to 23.8 per cent in 2001, and the Gini coefficient of inequality was 32 in 2005, a bit higher than the EU-15 average of 30 and much higher than the value in Finland (26).[3]

In addition, there is evidence that public services are of low quality in Ireland, especially health (low quality of care and inequality in access to health services) and education, generating strong inequalities in life-chances. Ireland also has more homeless people than many other European countries (Kirby, 2010) and homelessness doubled between 1993 and 2005.

The third weakness outlined by Kirby is the wrong adjustment to globalisation. Ireland is one of the most globalised countries in the world, but this adjustment came through the liberalisation of the banking sector and housing markets which led to even more exposure during the financial crisis.

Overall, the industrial policy chosen by the Irish state focused on attracting FDI by liberalising the economy and providing favourable tax rates at the expense of social cohesion. Thus Cullen (2004) shows the high price in health, quality of life and the social environment paid by Irish people for the economic boom.

Irish industrial policy has therefore not been sustainable from a social point of view. In terms of our sundial, the preferred levers have been innovation, knowledge, and provisions but not entitlements. Provisions have been favoured at the expense of entitlements, with capabilities increased only for a small (highly-skilled) part of the population.

Perhaps because of a lack of attention to entitlements in the whole population, FDI has not produced much spillover to the rest of the economy. Some studies have shown that the contribution of multinationals to the Irish economy has been small compared to their Irish revenues (see the review by Bailey et al., 2010a). Bailey et al. (2010a) conclude that there is evidence of Lewis-type dualism, in that indigenous firms have not benefited much from FDI. The evidence concerning the linkages between FDI and indigenous firms shows very small linkages in traditional and overall manufacturing sectors and significant but small linkages in the high-tech sector. Clusters have also developed in the country but their linkages with multinationals are low.

Bailey et al. (2010a) conclude that it is also important to develop domestic capabilities for industrial development, in order to avoid vulnerability. The Irish FDI-led growth has proved to be extremely vulnerable to both a downturn in the US economy and to a move of multinationals' activities to lower cost countries.

In 2008 the Irish government issued a recovery strategy entitled 'Building Ireland's Smart Economy' (Government of Ireland, 2008), which presented the government's industrial policy objectives for the next five years. The main objectives are to prepare the ground for recovery and long-term future growth, through two major sets of policies. The first set is just a continuation of previous Irish industrial policies, namely to spur the high-tech sector by attracting FDI, essentially by maintaining the competitiveness of the economy (through low taxes and low wages). The second set of policies aims at addressing environmental problems, making Ireland a 'green economy'.

The Irish experience shows in particular that focusing on one sector or one type of sector is not sustainable in the long-term. In fact, industrial policy in Ireland has been almost entirely focused on the high-tech sector, generating two problems:

1. the Irish high-tech sector has developed primarily thanks to foreign-owned firms butwith limited growth of indigenous firms;

2. it has produced a dual society where one part of the population, highly skilled workers in the high-tech sectors, are well-off while the rest of the population face unemployment because traditional and other lower-skill sectors have not developed much.

A knowledge-based economy should not only mean innovation capability in high-tech sectors but also access to knowledge and to learning mechanisms for all citizens in all sectors of the economy. Our sundial expresses just that: new sectors are needed but they should not constitute the only focus of industrial policy. In addition, developing a domestic capability for industrial development is very important to avoid vulnerability. However, developing domestic capability is generally a slow process that requires decades.

The Irish case also shows that industrial policy must be aligned with macroeconomic policies: a policy of tax relief for foreign firms locating in the country, together with moderate wage increases negotiated with social partners in order to further attract foreign firms, in exchange for income tax rebates, is inevitably accompanied by reduced public expenditure. If public expenditure does not go down in the area of infrastructure (essential to attract FDI) and innovation and training programmes for the sectors of the foreign firms (high-tech in Ireland), it has to go down in other areas. In Ireland, it has gone down in the area of social security.

FINLAND

As a result of a very deep recession in the early 1990s, it is argued that Finland has shifted from a resource-based to a knowledge-based economy in ten to 15 years, thanks to a strong and efficient research and technological development policy.

Looking at Finland's industrial story in more detail is illuminating. Not only did Finland rapidly move to a knowledge-based economy, but it also rapidly industrialised, shifting from an economy where the primary sector is predominant to an economy where the secondary sector prevails. In the 1950s, more than half the population and 40 per cent of output were still in the primary sector. Already by the 1970s the country become a mature industrial economy.

How did this happen? The evidence is that Finland's industrialisation was strongly backed by the state, through industrial policy.

From the 1950s on it started a policy of strong capital accumulation, where the state promoted, in agreement with business and other stakeholders, investments in two specific industrial sectors, forest and metal-based industries. The social consensus on this industrial policy appears to have been particularly strong, since many scholars stress its importance (for instance, Jäntti and Vartiainen, 2009; Ylä-Antilla and Palmberg, 2007).

The Finnish industrial development path was boosted and sustained by a number of elements. First, large investments could be made thanks to the high level of savings available in the economy. Public savings were high in Finland in the 1960s and 1970s by international standards, at about 8 per cent of GDP. These savings were used to finance investment and support state-owned firms in the basic-metal, chemical-fertilisers and energy sectors.

Second, interest rates were controlled by credit rationing. As a result of these first two elements, investment as a percentage of GDP was about 25 per cent in the 1960s and 35 per cent in the 1980s. A third element was the importance given to international linkages from the start. Finland being a small economy (just over 5 million people), it turned early towards exports in order to increase the extent of its market. Exports grew from about 20 per cent of GDP in 1960 to 30 per cent of GDP at the beginning of the twenty-first century.

A fourth element was the complementarity between sectors of the economy. In the industrialisation phase, the Finnish forest and metal industries grew in a complementary manner; in the later phase of transformation into a knowledge-based economy, the development of the different industries was also complementary since the main growing sector, information and communications technology (ICT), was also the driving-force for the modernisation of the more traditional industries.

A fifth element was the previously mentioned corporatism – a pragmatic and strong level of cooperation between the state, businesses and other stakeholders. 'The Finnish business elites colluded to distort the markets in a way that sustained high investment rates' (Jäntti and Vartiainen, 2009, p. 9). These two authors argue that the credibility of politicians is key in order to make industrial policy (growth policy for them) function: they have to have clear objectives, share them with businesses and workers, and set out a strategy to reach them.

Complementary to the fifth element, has been the low levels of corruption and a widely shared consensus across the population due to the nearby presence of the USSR, now Russia. The threat of the USSR appears to have made the Finnish more apt to consensus (Jäntti and Vartiainen, 2009): the country had to grow in order to justify its independence and workers had to be cared for in order to avoid increasing support for communist ideas and the possible influence of its neighbour country. Therefore, trade unions were encouraged to take part in the discussions on industrial policy and unionisation was encouraged.

Economic growth and industrial development therefore took place alongside social cohesion. Moderate wage increases were agreed in the negotiations between the state, businesses and labour in order to maintain the international competitiveness of Finnish firms. However, in return, the state committed to develop welfare services. For example, the expansion of the welfare system in the 1960s and 1970s led to the number of social workers tripling between 1970 and 1985. Health and other welfare services have been provided on the basis of universal access – access to all at the same price.

Industrial transformations and restructuring always generate winners and losers; when the government agrees with labour to favour certain transformations because they are the only guarantee of the country's long-term industrial development, but ensures that the losers will get support, it is more likely not only to get political consensus on the transformations but also to enable more people to take part in learning dynamics and become winners of industrial development.

Market forces alone do not consider losers' compensation, because of their focus on short-term profits. Only a political action can take this issue into account, because it brings benefits in the short term to the wider aim of economic development over and above income growth; and in the long-term, also to economic growth, by enabling more workers to take part in the new industrial development path through retraining programmes.

Finland is now a knowledge-based economy, after a second industrial transformation from 1990 onwards. To give just one example, the value of ICT export products was 5 per cent of Finland's total export value in 1990 and about 20 per cent in 1998 (Paija, 2000). In addition, according to international classifications, Finland is the country most specialised in ICT and has a high quality of education at all levels but especially at higher ones.

After the industrialisation phase of the 1950s to 1970s, Finland continued developing by looking to new industries. After the recession of the early-1990s, Finns agreed on a new social pact to restructure into a knowledge-based economy, building a national system of innovation, priority to research and development investment, clusters, and an ICT-driven industrial development path.

A quick look into the transformation of Finland into a knowledge-based economy shows that the industrial development strategy did not start in the 1990s but much earlier. A determining factor appears to be the adoption by the Finnish government, in the 1970s, of specific telecommunication standards that were subsequently adopted in other Nordic countries, and then Europe and the rest of the world. The international adoption of Finnish standards or of standards already adopted by Finnish firms provided them with a first mover advantage that was a key factor in their success.

Another specific aspect is that this move to a knowledge-based economy, through the rapid growth of the ICT sector, has been driven by one large firm that, given the small size of the Finnish economy, drove the whole industrial development of the country. This firm is of course Nokia, a very old Finnish firm created in 1865, which had run different businesses up to its specialisation in ICT in the 1990s (Ali-Yrkkö, 2001). Nokia developed its business in telecoms equipment and subsequently a cluster of smaller ICT firms developed in the country. In 1998, Nokia had about 300 first-tier suppliers. The Finnish ICT cluster now consists of thousands of firms, many of which used to work for Nokia but developed their independence and started supplying other firms, especially foreign ICT firms such as IBM, ICL (now Fujitsu-Siemens) and Ericsson.

However, Nokia is still the dominant actor in this business in Finland. It is the largest company in Finland, accounting for about a third of the market capitalisation of the national stock exchange. It represented about 3.3 per cent of the value of Finnish GDP, contributed 1.9 per cent to GDP growth and more than 30 per cent of the whole research and development (private and public) expenditure of the country in 2000 (Ali-Yrkkö, 2001). In contrast, it represented only 1.1 per cent of total Finnish employment, showing that new sectors such as ICT are useful to bring dynamism to economies but are not necessarily large employers. They predominantly employ highly-skilled employees who only represent a small part of the population. Hence the social sustainability of such an industrial policy strategy must also consider other sectors which can generate more employment at lower skill levels.

Nokia is a large *domestic* firm so the reliance of Finnish industrial development on one single large firm is not as worrying as in the case of Ireland, where large foreign-owned firms have come looking for high-tech skills but are ready to move if the relative costs of the same skills are lower in other countries. However, Finnish authorities are concerned about the lack of entrepreneurship in Finland, and are taking measures to promote it.

A number of lessons can be drawn from the Finnish case. First, a long-term perspective is necessary in order to design an appropriate industrial development path, and measures towards it must be consistent over time. Second, some specific sectors can be pin-pointed but the rest of the industrial structure must be considered too, and induced to restructure and adjust by favouring complementarities between sectors. In Finland, mature industries such as forestry and metals restructured by adopting new information and communications technologies to improve production processes.

CONCLUSIONS

This chapter has briefly illustrated the application of a holistic approach to industrial policy. It has also shown the heterogeneity in countries, and regions' initial conditions and possible paths to industrial development. Each country has specific economic, social and political history and conditions and has to define specific development strategies.

The holistic approach not only means defining appropriate measures to guide effective development along an appropriate path, but also to hold the different parts in a coherent whole, in a dynamic way, maintaining coherence as the whole evolves and grows.

Among the countries considered, it appears that those which have paid attention to social cohesion as well as training, education and investment to favour the restructuring of traditional industries and the development of new industries (for example, Finland), have performed best. Finland, although a small country with limited resources, has managed to develop a sustainable industrial development path built on consensus and coherent actions on the social side (training, education and welfare) and on the economic side (investment in research and development, and regional development). Brazil also appears to have chosen a balanced development path and a set of coherent measures, although our analysis of this country is too brief to provide detailed evidence.

Ireland appears to have chosen a vulnerable industrial development path, paying little attention to social cohesion and choosing a high dependence on foreign multinationals rather than developing a strong domestic industrial base.

China is an example of development fuelled by an enormous growth of provisions without entitlements. In fact, only very high growth rates can make such a development path sustainable.

South Africa is a country where entitlements have been extended but provisions remain unequally distributed, thereby preventing a part of the population really taking part in development.

Industrial development strategies therefore vary according to history, as well as social, economic and political characteristics. They have to be coherent in order to be sustainable, not only between different policy areas (social, welfare, innovation and trade, for example), but also between policy levels (local, regional and national).

The next chapter shows how the EU has been able to define a coherent industrial policy, not only between policy areas, since treaties have constantly stressed the importance of coherence between policy fields (at least since the Maastricht Treaty), but also between policy levels which, in the EU, are not only regional and national, but also supranational.

NOTES

1. One of these experts was Patrizio Bianchi who was economic adviser to the Governor of the Guangdong province in 2000.
2. The promised tax rebate in return for lower wages is put into question by O'Toole (1997), who shows that employees on 50 per cent of the average industrial wage rate saw the average tax rate rise from 14.4 per cent in 1980 to 17.4 per cent in 1995, while employees on five times the average industrial wage saw their average tax rate decline from 50.6 per cent in 1980 to 46.8 per cent in 1995.
3. Source: Eurostat http://appsso.eurostat.ec.europa.eu/nui/show.do?dataset=ilc_sic2&lang=en.

6. The European experience

In 2000, the EU launched a complex strategy for industrial development aiming to revitalize the European economy by completing the three phase process establishing monetary union and enlargement to Central and Eastern European countries. The context external to the EU was also important since the Doha trade agreement was signed in the same year and China entered the World Trade Organization (WTO). The Lisbon Strategy proposed concerted action involving multiple policies and represented a long-term vision of industrial development for the EU.

This chapter explores how this new approach relates to previous European approaches to industrial policy. First, a historical review of industrial policy is provided, based on our previous work (Bianchi and Labory, 2009). The Lisbon Strategy is then analysed as a long-term vision of industrial development. The problem with this strategy has been the lack of political commitment to its implementation, as we will see in this chapter.

ECONOMIC OPENING AND STRUCTURAL ADJUSTMENT POLICIES

Economic union means an aggregation of nation states agreeing a series of common rules in order to guide an economic integration process. Economic union is therefore primarily a political action that facilitates an institutional transformation and, with it, structural dynamics within and between countries.

In order to define the nature and direction of the structural changes brought about by the opening of the economy it is therefore necessary to simultaneously define the collective dynamics and institutional changes: that is the collective norms that regulate the internal and external relationships of the social groups that interact through the economic opening process.

Historically, up to the beginning of the economic integration process, European capitalism developed within each nation; each European country implementing its own strong industrial policies to support national champions. The extent of national sovereignty was more limited than the extent of the market, with the consequence that economic growth inevitably turned into a conflict of nations.

The productive system was defined on a national basis so that the state could act on the division of labour and on the extent of the market. Interventions on the division of labour aimed at concentrating production; interventions on the extent of the market aimed at opening foreign markets through trade policy.

The traditional references of that industrial policy have been France's strong interventionism, as well as the Japanese experience of the Ministry of International Trade and Industry (MITI): that is, strong central bureaucracies that could define and orient effective economic development towards specific industrial development paths using command-and-control instruments together with a strong moral orientation of independent economic agents.

This vision of interventionist industrial policy did not leave space for competition policy. Instead the state was pushing to concentrate national industry in order to reach scale efficiencies and be well-equipped to compete in world markets, defending national interests. This type of policy was also characterised by its centralisation and consequent neglect of local development issues, apart from issues related to factor prices.

This policy perspective cannot function in an economic integration process, such as a tariff and economic union. At the beginning the integration process may function, leaving national institutions and interest groups unchanged. However, as integration proceeds national alliances are inevitably questioned by the structural changes brought about and new alliances get created that pull together interests from across national boundaries.

Integration inevitably has an effect on national institutions, and common rules must be defined in order to avoid national interests requesting protection. The politically crucial and delicate step of the economic integration process therefore consists of defining the transition towards an economic union and setting out the policy approach to favour the structural changes that have to take place in order for the process to be effective.

INDUSTRIAL POLICY IN THE TREATY OF ROME

The absence of explicit provisions regarding industrial policy in the Treaty of Rome was not the result of neglect but of a clear limit imposed by national governments on the powers of the Community.

The conception of industrial policy was that of a central authority which, through the specification of administrative acts, classified firm behaviour as forbidden or admissible – or to be promoted – in order to reach an industrial structure that was assessed as most in line with the general objectives. This conception of industrial policy has been called 'constructivist' and is of French origin, having been developed during the reign of Louis XIV by his Minister of Finance, Jean-Baptiste Colbert. It presupposed that the state had the technical capacities and the political legitimacy to delineate and manage objectives of national development and collective welfare using regulatory instruments. It was still the prevalent approach to industrial policy in France in the 1950s operated by the Commissariat Général au Plan, the head of which was Jean Monnet.

The basic principle of such an approach is that the extent of the market is wider than the area of sovereignty of the national state and so the government must 'guide' its industry to make the country economically independent and politically strong.

The authority governing industry therefore has a political role which can only be assigned to the central government. The assignment of such functions to a supranational government could only arise in exceptional cases, where codetermination principles could be accepted in the name of collective welfare. In other words, given possible economic conflicts that would eventually become political, the European states accepted the idea of creating a common organisation that would govern production and trade in order to internalise these possible conflicts.

As a result the Treaty of Rome only contains rules about fair competition in the common market, while industrial policy is left to the authority of national governments. The treaty does however contain the objective of stable industrial development, to avoid internal divergence that could put common action at risk. The treaty also includes precise norms that prevent nation states from implementing any public interventions that would create obstacles to the functioning of the common market.

The main action in favour of industrial development was in fact the completion of the tariff and economic union that the Treaty of Rome instituted. This process of integrating the economies of the six founding countries was set up to allow the necessary structural adjustments to take place in a progressive manner. Member states could take measures to promote structural adjustment and also measures to strengthen national firms so that they could compete in the new common market. The main measures included in the Treaty of Rome regarding competition in the common market therefore concern fair competition and preventing the abuse of dominant positions (as well as cartels and any implicit or explicit agreements), and the prohibition of state aid that favours national firms at the expense of firms in other member states.

Exceptions were allowed that enabled the implementation of industrial policy in practice. For example, Article 85(3) of the Treaty of Rome allowed derogations to the prohibition of cartels or any agreement between firms in the case of agreements aiming to improve production or product distribution, or to promote technical or economic progress, provided they did not end up restricting competition in the common market.

This formulation was a compromise between the French and the German visions of the time. The French vision favoured fusions and acquisitions to create national champions and did not include competition as a key objective. The German vision paid attention to the fair functioning of markets, although actions aimed at improving social aspects were also considered necessary.

So while the abuse of dominant positions was prohibited, exceptions were allowed where considered necessary for technical progress and for ensuring the competitiveness of European firms against outside firms, primarily large American firms.

EUROPEAN INDUSTRIAL POLICY IN THE 1970s

In the 1970s industrial policy fell within the competence of member states, although within the framework defined at the European level. The crises of the 1970s hit the various member states differently. The Community took a supervisory role when it came to national policies but also explicitly promoted constructivist policies. The most obvious illustration of this was in the steel sector, where

Commissioner Davignon proposed a plan for the restructuring of the sector based on agreed market shares and determined minimum prices (May 1977). This plan was accompanied by subsidies to firms in order for them to reduce their production capacity.

This action plan conducted within the European Coal and Steel Community generated similar actions in other sectors: an agreement between the 11 main European producers of synthetic fibres was signed in 1978. This split the European market on the basis of the market shares prevailing in 1976, and introduced subsidies and protectionist trade policy measures limiting imports from outside the Community. Thus the Commission itself interpreted its role in industrial development in the 1970s as a guarantee of the competitiveness of European firms in the face of foreign rivals, even if this could slow down their structural adjustment.

The promotion of agreements between firms and subsidy provision have in fact delayed the necessary structural adjustment of European firms, thereby slowing down the economic integration process. The situation reached an extreme in the early 1980s when the term 'Eurosclerosis' was coined to define the European economy.

Consequently the 1980s saw the relaunch of the economic integration process based on the idea that completing the internal market was in itself the main industrial policy to adopt. This meant abandoning the protection of national firms and implementing European competition policy more strictly, alongside a less protective trade policy.

To promote the competitiveness of European firms, industrial policy shifted to regional and local levels, with the new aim of improving the capacity of firms to take part in competitive markets by providing the right conditions rather than providing subsidies that compensated for their inefficiencies but also delayed their structural adjustment.

INDUSTRIAL POLICY IN THE SINGLE EUROPEAN ACT AND IN THE TREATY ON THE EUROPEAN UNION

The constructivist approach to industrial policy was therefore progressively abandoned in the 1980s in favour of an evolutionary approach more in line with the German tradition, adopted implicitly in the Single European Act (1986) and explicitly and fully in the Maastricht Treaty (1992).

This approach was announced by different initiatives and defined in the Bangemann Report.[1] This was a key document as it defined the new approach to industrial policy. Community action should aim to create a context favourable to the competitiveness of firms rather than directly acting on firms (with subsidies for instance) to preserve their efficiency. Creating the appropriate framework or context has meant both ensuring the good functioning of the common market and acting as a catalyst and pioneer of industrial development. This has been accomplished through the promotion of research and technological development, training and human capital improvement, the promotion of the development of SMEs, and the development of service and industrial cooperation networks.

The Maastricht Treaty adopted this approach. It contains, for the first time in European treaties, an explicit article on the opportunity to implement policies for the development of industrial competitiveness: article 130 defines the extent of European industrial policy. In addition to article 130, numerous provisions complete the definition of the new industrial policy approach: article 130F on innovation and research policy; article 129 on infrastructure networks; as well as provisions on environment and competition policies and measures to promote the completion of the internal market.

Industrial policy in an open and competitive context was thus defined, consisting of various actions aimed at both increasing the extent of the market and accelerating firms' organisational and technological adjustment. This vision of industrial policy was based on a set of instruments which aimed to create the conditions for social development and collective growth.

The Maastricht Treaty thus proposed a method for industrial policy that combined the common approach with the intergovernmental approach. Article 130 claims that 'the Member States shall consult each other in liaison with the Commission and, where necessary, shall coordinate their actions. The Commission may take any useful initiative to promote such coordination . . .. The Parliament shall be kept fully informed'.

This approach to industrial policy had wide implications as its design could be implemented beyond the EU's borders as a design of industrial policy in an open economy. The approach was successful because it was compatible with the liberal approach of most governments at that time, primarily the US and international organisations recommending the 'Washington Consensus' recipe to promote growth in developing countries. The term industrial policy was even abandoned because it was taken to mean the direct intervention of the state in markets. Rather, the term competitiveness policy was preferred, emphasising the horizontal approach to provide the conditions for businesses to prosper with limited state intervention.

EUROPEAN INDUSTRIAL POLICY IN THE TWENTY-FIRST CENTURY

Despite this approach, there was a constant competitiveness gap between the EU and its main rivals Japan and the US in the 1990s – especially in the development of high-tech sectors. Europe appeared to have the capacity to innovate but not to transform innovation into commercial success. European firms also appeared less able to adopt new technologies, especially information and communication technologies, which has prevented them from increasing productivity (see Bianchi and Labory, 2009, Chapter 9 and 10). In addition, by the end of the 1990s and early 2000s, European firms were also challenged by firms from emerging economies, such as China, India, Korea, Singapore and Taiwan.

As a consequence, the debate on industrial policy emerged again in the EU at the beginning of the new century, especially in 2002 when member states became concerned about the deindustrialisation of the EU. In 2003 and 2004 the European Commission published two reports analysing the process of deindustrialisation in the EU and concluded that it was not a real threat for two major reasons. First, deindustrialisation is in fact 'tertiarisation' of the economy, whereby services take growing importance. This phenomenon is not worrying for industry as most new services are related to manufacturing activities and offer the opportunity to reorganise production, and create global value chains. Second, the delocalisation of manufacturing activities to countries outside the EU, another aspect of deindustrialisation, should not create problems as long as the EU remains a worldwide centre of excellence for human capital and innovative capacity.

The reports stressed two main problems for European industry.

On the one hand, the productivity gap with the US continued to widen. On the other hand, the performance of European high-tech sectors vis-à-vis rivals in the US, Japan and emerging countries was not satisfactory. The Lisbon Strategy was supposed to address these problems.

THE LISBON STRATEGY

In 2000, EU member states met in Lisbon with the President of the European Commission, Romano Prodi, and defined a long-term strategy which aimed at 'making the Union the most competitive and dynamic knowledge-based economy of the world, capable of sustainable economic growth thanks to job creation and rising social cohesion, by the year 2010'. In order to reach this objective, the EU needed to develop innovation and an information society, streamline the European social model, and guarantee good macroeconomic conditions with an appropriate policy mix. The strategy proposed six measures:

1. the e-Europe action plan, to develop an information society through measures to use the internet in government and public services and favour competition in the telecommunication sector to ensure lower connection prices;
2. the creation of the European Area of Research and Innovation, focusing on a better coordination of innovative activities within the EU, strengthening relationships between business and academia, the promotion of researchers' mobility, and the creation of a European patent;
3. support to SMEs and to firm creation by reducing start-up costs and by promoting innovation;
4. the completion of the internal market, especially in financial and other services;
5. the promotion of efficient and integrated financial markets with particular attention to SMEs' access to financial capital;
6. the coordination of macroeconomic policies.

The European Commission was assigned the role of coordinating national policies and monitoring the progress made towards the achievement of the objectives. The European Commission subsequently defined a new approach to European policymaking, called the 'open coordination method'. Member states were invited to exchange information on the measures they had implemented so that best practice could be identified and adopted elsewhere, thereby creating partnerships between member states under the monitoring of the European Commission.

The Lisbon Strategy is therefore an industrial policy in the wide sense of the term – a long-term vision that should at least start to bring all member states to the same industrial and economic development path. The strategy has been criticised as incoherent, due in particular to the contradiction between the necessity for public support to research and development and innovation – requiring an increase in funds, like the other micro policies suggested by the strategy – and the requirements of macroeconomic stability, especially within the eurozone, which requires budget constraint. However, we think the main problem here is that of EMU, not of the Lisbon Strategy *per se*. EMU membership imposes strict budget criteria and thereby limits the possibility that countries can implement fiscal policies favouring economic growth. This problem was not resolved but rather brought to the extreme during the Greek crisis at the beginning of 2010, mentioned in Chapter 1.

The idea of a long-term strategy defined at the European level that member states subsequently adapt and implement in their own countries seems to be appropriate. States can decide on the best instruments to adopt after consulting with others and company best practice. Member states can also coherently define regional development strategies.

The problem is that in recent years member states have tended to play independently and without considering the collective benefits within the EU. The crises of 2001–2002 and of 2008 have shown how selfish member states are, in the sense of lacking a political will to pursue the European integration process. The difficulties of ratifying the Lisbon Treaty provides additional evidence of this lack of political will. Citizens might be reluctant to pursue the integration process and therefore do not vote in favour of it; but the main fault lies with politicians who do not carry out appropriate information campaigns that would convince European citizens of the benefits of pursuing the integration process further.

All too often, the EU level is presented nationally as the external constraint that imposes unpopular measures. One example is the restrictive fiscal policy proposed in June 2010 by the Italian government which was presented as being imposed by the European integration process and the speculative attacks of financial markets, about which the government had no room for manoeuvre. The result is that the EU is increasingly negatively perceived by European citizens.

The failure of the Lisbon Strategy is therefore primarily political and due to the current political crisis of the EU. In fact the European Commission claims in 2006, in its strategy for European innovation policy, that 'today Europe does not need new commitments; it needs political leadership and decisive actions' (European Commission, 2006, p. 3).

Consequently the EU, with the Lisbon Strategy, has defined a specific European approach to industrial policy, coordinating both a wide set of instruments and a wide set of implementation levels. The long-term vision of industrial development to which all member states adhere is defined on the European level, not by the Commission on its own but essentially on the basis of a dialogue between member states in the European Council. The long-term vision is then implemented by all policy decision-making levels from the European to the local levels.

The main level for competence is the national one, where each country adapts the strategy to its own needs and conditions, and takes the necessary measures. At the EU level, the Commission monitors progress towards the general objectives and coordinates national efforts, promoting an exchange of information and experiences between European countries. The Commission also coordinates efforts made at the local level, supporting the sharing of experiences between regions for instance through the Interreg programme. The 'open coordination method' adopted by the Commission is very important in ensuring coherence at the European level as well as leaving room in the future for, possibly, a more important role for the EU in defining and implementing industrial policy.

This new approach is therefore the natural evolution of the Bangemann approach, taking a more active role in the orientation of industrial specialisation in the EU and in bringing about structural change to follow specific paths. While in the 1990s industrial policy was aimed at providing the conditions for industry to embark on the best path, in the 2000s public authorities at all levels also try to identify the best path in order to orient industrial development towards it.

A FRAMEWORK FOR THE ANALYSIS OF INDUSTRIAL POLICY AS A LONG-TERM VISION OF INDUSTRIAL DEVELOPMENT

In this section, we synthesise the evolution of European industrial policy and pull out some key elements, using our framework for analysing industrial policy in a long-term perspective.

Overall, three phases of industrial policy can be identified, which we present in a stylised manner in Table 6.1. The table identifies the main elements of the industrial policies implemented in each phase. In the first phase, industrial policies were selective and interventionist. Actions could be distinguished according to the type of industry. Traditional, crisis industries were sustained by subsidies

Table 6.1   Phases of the evolution of European industrial policy

	Phase 1 (1970s and 1980s)	Phase 2 (Bangemann)	Phase 3 (Lisbon)
Actions	– Subsidies to old industry – National champions – Protection of infant industry	– Actions on the context, the competitive environment (antitrust and regulation; action at territorial level) – Development of new industry: innovation as development of new technology	– Providing fair rules – Development of new industry: knowledge – Innovation as knowledge accumulation and creation – Complex interactions at territorial but also wider levels: networks
Levers	Entitlements Provisions	Entitlements Provisions Innovation Territory	Entitlements Provisions Innovation Territory
Approach	Traditional approaches to industrial policy	Horizontal approaches to industrial policy	Dynamic approach to industrial policy: stress on cumulativeness and sustainability

or state ownership. Other industries were sustained by promoting international competitiveness, helping them to create and adopt new technologies or guarantee markets (through public procurement). New industries were promoted through infant industry protection, namely protection from foreign trade in the first stages of their existence. Industrial policy acted on the rules of the competitive game with trade policy, regulation and competition policy, although the latter was not strongly implemented in Europe in that phase. The other lever of industrial development on which industrial policy action was concentrated was resources, namely provisions. Extending provisions meant guaranteeing the availability of the necessary resources for development: human capital, financial capital and raw materials. Entitlements were also important, since each country implemented social cohesion and welfare policies and the European social model consolidated in that period.

In the second phase, defined at the European level by the approach set out by Commissioner Bangemann in his famous report (1990), industrial policy was no longer based on direct intervention but on providing the conditions for industrial development. This meant that entitlements were even more stressed than in the previous phase, since the approach left the market to function on its own and fair competition and firm creation had to be guaranteed by the availability of provisions and entitlements, allowing all individuals to take part in the competitive game.

This approach differs from that of the first phase not only because of the elements of provisions and entitlements, but also, and more fundamentally, due to the addition of two additional levers: innovation and territory. Given the increasing gap in performance between American, Japanese and European firms, innovation is considered an essential (dynamic) lever for the competitiveness of European firms – hence the strengthening of the framework programme and technology policy in the EU, explicitly formalised in the Maastricht Treaty.

Last, but not least, the new approach recognised that industrial development primarily arises at the local level, in specific territories where synergies and proximity make knowledge accumulation, exchange and creation possible, thereby allowing firm creation and growth. Bottom-up approaches therefore substituted the top-down approaches of the earlier phase. The representation of the key levers of industrial development are shown in Figure 6.1. All levers have to be considered for industrial development to be sustainable.

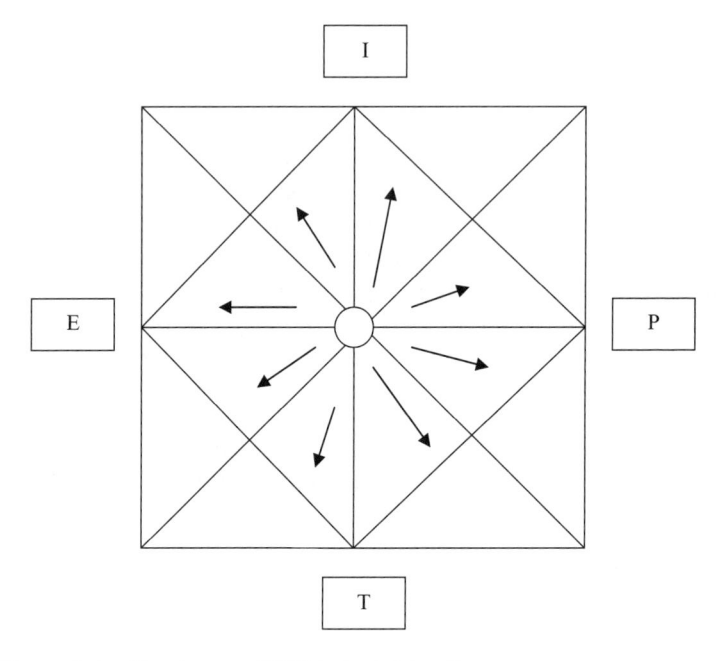

Figure 6.1 Key levers of EU industrial policy

Notice that this framework is not fixed but dynamic: innovation allows firm creation that embeds in territories and enables social cohesion to develop; in turn this allows entitlements to consolidate, and innovation is strengthened and promoted since more people take part in the learning mechanisms contributing to the development process.

In the third phase, beginning with the launch of the Lisbon Strategy, a new approach to industrial policy is progressively defined and implemented. This tries to take into account the fall of the Berlin Wall and the end of the bipolar world, the emergence of new powers, especially in Asia, and technological developments that spur the knowledge-based economy. The levers are the same but have to be extended further; for instance, territory includes a wider emphasis on the environment.

CONCLUSIONS

In 2010 a new strategy has been defined by the EU for the period 2010 to 2020 to replace the Lisbon Strategy.[2] The strategy is defined as a growth strategy, and is concerned with overall economic growth. The development path chosen is one defined as smart, sustainable and inclusive, and is based on knowledge and innovation, the need to preserve the environment' and including everyone in the development process to ensure social cohesion.

One of the elements necessary to achieve these objectives is industrial policy. The European Commission defines industrial policy as enterprise policy, namely measures aimed at firms. This is a rather restrictive definition of industrial policy compared to the broader one we adopt in this book. In this book we have talked about industrial policy as industrial development policy, in a vision that sees industrial policy as an instrument to wider economic, social and cultural development. For this purpose, a holistic approach is necessary that considers not only the specific part, namely the industry and the firms within it, but also the whole of which the industry is a part, because the industry does not develop if the whole is not compatible. Other parts of the whole include social cohesion, which determines income distribution in the population and the propensity to consume industry's products; education and training which determines the skills available to industry; and university research which also offers technological development opportunities to firms.

A key element of the 2020 strategy is human capital, because it is fundamental to create and maintain learning processes. Human capital, together with territorial assets such as social capital, are indeed key to knowledge-creation processes such as innovation. Industrial development must involve not only a single high-tech sector, but also other traditional or more mature sectors that also employ many workers. These workers have to be appropriately trained and involved in labour division in order for learning processes to arise also in these industries. Social cohesion is thus essential to a sustainable industrial development path, because it is complementary and expands learning processes to the whole economy. Social cohesion also allows cultural and civil development, which are the basis for the additional learning processes.

Provisions, entitlements, innovation and territory must be developed in a balanced and complementary manner in order for industrial development to take place and be maintained. The actions needed to create and maintain these learning processes are many, from education and training to research and development, and from particular support for green technologies to competition and open trade provisions. Appropriate actions must be implemented at all levels of policymaking, including regional, national and supranational levels. The coherence between the different levels of decision-making are also emphasised in the 2020 strategy.

This new European industrial policy thus essentially becomes a vision of the future, towards which various policies implemented by policymakers at all levels could be coherently orientated.

The new industrial policy necessarily recalls an articulated vision of the economy or, as Hirschman (1999) would argue, is a way of making the economy more complex. This strategy indeed implies a complex and multi-layered vision of the state, from the EU to towns. The role of the European level is to define a long-term strategy, implement common programmes that create European networks, and regulate the competitive environment. The national level defines and implements industrial policies to support the participation of individuals and firms in the competitive game, while the local and regional levels operate the territorial planning needed for development.

The success of this new approach will depend on the capacity of EU members to unify behind a common objective and eliminate national tensions that, especially in the context of a world crisis, tend to mistakenly focus on the national frontiers as the natural area where problems can be best resolved. As stressed by the European Commission in its communication proposing the 2020 strategy, 'Europe can succeed if it acts collectively, as a Union' (European Commission, 2010, p. 3). The EU strategy for 2020, if appropriately and convincingly implemented, could also constitute an effective industrial policy.

NOTES

1. COM(1990) 557 Final, 16 November 1990, 'Industrial policy in an open and competitive environment'.
2. Proposal by the European Commission (2010) adopted by the European Council in June 2010.

Conclusions

Deep structural transformations have occurred in economies and societies in the last 20 years, essentially as a result of globalisation. A debate on the usefulness of industrial policies started at the beginning of the new century, marking a sort of 'return' of industrial policies. The crisis has revealed how necessary this debate was, and is, for four major reasons.

First, the crisis has revealed that markets do not self-regulate and that the state has a role in helping this regulation.

Second, the crisis has revealed that long-term perspectives cannot be ignored. The crisis is, to a large extent, determined by the predominance of short-term views, despite what current behaviour may bring in the future. We have shown in this book that long-term perspectives, both in economic analyses and in policymaking, are essential in order for economic development to be sustainable, in the sense of having the capacity to self-generate resources for future growth and in the sense of guaranteeing social and environmental sustainability.

Third, the crisis has revealed that a political economy framework is useful in order to understand the complexity of the economic system and of industrial development, and to define appropriate economic policies. Isolating economic phenomena from political and social characteristics and dynamics only leads to policy failures. For instance, a policy for economic development that does not take account of the fact that a certain part of the population may be excluded from markets due to their social status will not be effective in spurring development, or at least will only lead to unbalanced and unsustainable development.

In the changed context of today's world the lessons of classical economists are more useful than ever. Of particular use is Adam Smith, who highlighted that the wealth of nations is primarily determined by industrial production, and the capacity to organise specialisations and complementarities in knowledge and competencies.

Classical economists taught that industrial production is efficient if it corresponds to a market where competition is the expression of the right of all individuals to autonomously and independently participate in collective action. The long term goal of autonomous and independent participation of all individuals in markets and industrial production, rather than the short term goals of immediate profits, are what drive the wealth of nations.

In this context, new industrial policies imply a new design of the international regulatory system. This includes not only a redefinition of the role of international institutions, but also the search for new development goals that take the problems that the global economy has to face into account, including the environment, health and food security. For this reason, thinking about industrial policy does not amount to thinking about a battery of incentives and protectionist measures to save the national economy, but rather to discuss the concept of the market and the state in a global context.

We therefore propose a framework for the definition of industrial policies, taking production organisation or, in Smith's words, labour division, as the unit of analysis. The key idea of this framework is that industrial policy should act on the learning capacity of the economic system by activating appropriate gears towards certain development paths. The division of labour determines productivity by enabling the application of skill, dexterity and judgment on productive processes. In dynamic terms labour division allows learning, improvements and knowledge creation. We have shown that the deep structural transformations of the last 20 to 30 years, related to globalisation, have led to re-organisations of production such that the new productive processes are centred on knowledge, and hence on people. Indeed, the more heterogeneous is the 'work done', the more consistent should be the 'work to be done', namely the knowledge flows within the production process."

The division of labour determines the capacity of the industrial system to adapt to changes in the extent of the market, and so to bring about structural adjustments, which implies industrial development. Specific labour division adjustments are possible if both entitlements and provisions are adequate; that is, if people have the capabilities to take part in the competitive game and if rules of the game are adequately defined and guaranteed by the state.

A fourth major problem revealed by the crisis is therefore that these provisions and entitlements are no longer completely defined at the national level alone. A large part of these are now interdependent, and a countries' provisions and entitlements depend on decisions made by other countries. The economy is open because political and economic actors are increasingly interdependent, with decisions taken in one part of the world having a potential impact in other parts of the world.

Globalisation has a profound impact on the relationship between states and markets. Thirty years ago, when national capitalism was largely controlled by national governments, the spheres of capitalism and democracy coincided. Today, capitalism has become global while democracy remains at national or local level. Capitalism is ruled by a multi-level governance system, where some decisions are made in international institutions (such as the WTO and IMF, and also the International Accounting Standards Board regarding intangible asset reporting, and international patent offices), others by national and regional institutions, or by independent authorities. As stressed by Schmidt (2004), politics is largely at the national level, while policy (the activity of an authority with public power and institutional legitimacy) and polity (the way in which social parties which represent a policy organise and the way in which the authority organises) arise at international, national and local levels.

From the point of view of economic modelling, rationality and welfare-maximising policies presuppose the existence of a strong central authority and an economic and political system under control. Welfare-maximising policies can be defined at various levels of government, especially lower levels, but what about their effects on other levels? What is their interdependence with policies defined at other levels?

The economy is knowledge-based, perhaps as it has always been although it is more intensely so now. It is clear that technology and products are far more complicated nowadays than in the days of Adam Smith or Schumpeter. Consumers use cars, telephones and the internet, the functioning of which requires a degree in engineering to understand. Consumers buy medicines and food but are unable to say whether particular components or ingredients can be potentially harmful. Products therefore embody much greater knowledge than at the beginning of the twentieth century.

The consequences are twofold. First, production systems have changed. Their major distinguishing feature now, in our opinion, is their increasing reliance on intangible assets. We have argued that the higher knowledge content of goods implies a change in the value creation process of firms whereby pre- and post-manufacturing phases of production receive greater importance. These are the phases which are more intensive in intangible assets, namely human capital (in the sense of skills), knowledge and innovation, and social capital.

The ability to create and benefit from networks has become a key strategic asset, as value creation is governed and realised in global value chains. We argue in this book that the knowledge intensity of products, which makes intangible-intensive phases of the production process relatively more important, may be a factor in the offshoring of manufacturing production phases. This constitutes an important structural change in industrial systems, called 'the second unbundling' by Baldwin (2006).

When knowledge is the key asset in the economy, human capital is also fundamental. Knowledge and competencies are embodied in people who create knowledge collectively by communicating and exchanging knowledge and experiences. However, only people with a certain level of skills can take part in knowledge creation processes and become part of a firm's core workforce with long-term contracts.

People with relatively low levels of skills are pressured to take part in the knowledge creation process of the firm, at all levels. Employees dealing with purely technical tasks in the firm, for instance implementing administrative procedures or implementing software in machines, are also asked to identify problems and suggest improvements. Many studies have shown that stress has increased for many workers with medium levels of skills (not unskilled) as the new working practices have been implemented. Meanwhile, unskilled workers are left behind and paid very low wages with short-term contracts that cost the firm less.

Second, and following from the first point, it 'makes it more important than it has ever been before for everyone in society to be well-educated in their early years, and to have access to good, impartial sources of information throughout their lives' (Fleischaker, 2004, p. 268). The education system therefore becomes a key lever of industrial development and economic growth, especially at higher education levels and in particular universities, but also at lower levels.

Not everybody though can reach high skill levels. Specific labour legislation should therefore be defined for the unskilled, to give these people guarantees (at least against poverty) and a certain entitlement to take part in industrial development. Skilled workers must be educated not only technically, to obtain the knowledge necessary to perform specific tasks, but also behaviourally, to obtain the knowledge and competencies necessary to be able to communicate knowledge and take part in collective knowledge creation processes. Perhaps it is the latter aspect which makes tasks less 'offshorable'.

The role of universities has changed in the last decades, as universities increasingly take an active role in industrial development by encouraging firm creation and, more generally, the valorisation of the new knowledge created by its researchers. However, universities also maintain the fundamental role of educating people and forming the human capital necessary for industry. They enable firms to specialise in appropriate tasks, allowing them to either govern or be part of global value chains, without losing too much bargaining power to defend their position.

In addition, when knowledge rather than machines is key to firms' competitiveness and to industrial development, the wider goals of economic growth – those that were stressed by classical economists – take primary importance again. Knowledge creation and accumulation requires not only that people be skilled, with a certain knowledge base and specific competencies, but also that people have a certain level of culture and openness to exchange with other people. In other words, knowledge creation and accumulation requires a civilised society, in the sense given to the term by Dahrendorf (2008, p. 19): 'It is that in order to advance human welfare one needs both, entitlements and provisions. People need access to markets and politics and culture, but these universes also have to offer numerous and manifold choices. No society can be regarded as truly civilised that does not offer both'.

A civil society gives meaning to the ways in which people live together, providing equal opportunities to all and punishing illegal behaviour (justice). It also provides citizens with more than just material well-being, but also social well-being, solidarity and non-exclusion, and access to cultural development (happiness), which in turn feeds industrial and economic development.

Rethinking industrial policies today means redefining the basic concepts of collective actions and putting them in a dynamic perspective.

The crisis is not only financial, it is also the result of a vision of the world which tended to ignore the centrality of the link between production, knowledge and people in economic phenomena. In the 1990s and early years of the new century grew the conviction that knowledge increasingly was the engine of industrial and economic development, as shown by the much used and perhaps abused terms 'knowledge-based economy' or 'knowledge society'. As shown in Chapter 6, the European Union realised the challenge in 2000 by defining the Lisbon Strategy, which was however not fully implemented.

Knowledge essentially means people, who are rooted in specific territories, characterised by institutions and rules. Public action can accelerate knowledge creation and application by acting on two policy axes, innovation and territory on the one hand and entitlements and provisions on the other. In the globalised world characterised by unbundling, these two axes are important and especially the combination of entitlements and innovation, namely providing education in a sense of valorising people's rights. It is today necessary to find a new morality of the economy, as an instrument to favour the growth of resources, rights, participation and the responsibility of people, particularly in their labour, which remains the main engine of the "wealth of nations".

References

Alchian, A. and H. Demsetz (1972), 'Production, information costs and economic organisation', *American Economic Review*, **62**: 777–95.

Ali-Yrkkö, J. (2001), 'The role of Nokia in the Finnish economy', Research Institute of the Finnish Economy (ETLA), No.1, pp. 72–80.

Bacci, L. (ed.) (2004), *Distretti e imprese leader nel sistema Moda della Toscana*, Milan: Franco Angeli.

Bacci, L., S. Labory, and M. Lombardi (2010), 'The evolution of external linkages and relational density in the Tuscan leather industry', in F. Belussi and A. Sammarra (eds), *Business Networks in Clusters and Industrial Districts. The Governance of the Global Value Chain*, London and New York: Routledge, pp. 146–71.

Bailey, D. and K. Cowling (2006), 'Industrial policy and vulnerable capitalism', *International Review of Applied Economics*, **20**(5): 537–53.

Bailey, D., M. Bellandi, A. Caloffi and L. De Propris (2010a), 'Place-renewing leadership: trajectories of change for mature manufacturing regions in Europe', *Policy Studies*, **31** (4): 457–74.

Bailey, D., H. Lenihan and A. Singh (2010b), 'Tiger, tiger, burning bright? Industrial policy "lessons" from Ireland for small African economies', in J. Stiglitz (ed.), *Africa Task Force Initiative for public Dialogue Volume I*, Oxford: Oxford University Press.

Baldwin, R. (2006), 'Globalisation: the great unbundling', Prime Minister's Office, Economic Council of Finland, accessed 9 November 2010 at www.graduateinstitute.ch/webdav/site/ctei/shared/CTEI/Baldwin/Publications/Chapters/Globalization/Baldwin_06-09-20.pdf.

Bianchi, P. (1981), *Produzione e potere di mercato*, Rome: Ediesse.

Bianchi, P. and S. Labory (eds) (2004), *The Economic Importance of Intangible Assets*, London: Ashgate.

Bianchi, P. and S. Labory (2006a), 'Empirical evidence on industrial policy using state aid data', *International Review of Applied Economics*, **20**(5): 603–22.

Bianchi, P. and S. Labory (2006b), 'From old industrial policy to new industrial development policies: an introduction', in P. Bianchi and S. Labory (eds), *International Handbook of Industrial Policy*, Cheltenham, UK and Northampton, MA, USA: Edward Elgar, pp. 3–27.
Bianchi, P. and S. Labory (2009), *Le nuove politiche industriali dell'Unione europea*, Bologna: Il Mulino.
Bianchi, P. and S. Labory (2010), 'Economic crisis and industrial policy', *Revue d'économie industrielle*, **129–30**: 301–26.
Black, S. and L. Lynch (1997), 'How to compete: the impact of workplace practices and information technology on productivity', National Bureau of Economic Research working paper series, no. 6120.
Burlamaqui, L. (2000), 'Evolutionary economics and the economic role of the state', in L. Burlamaqui, A-C. Castro and H-J. Chang (eds), *Institutions and the Role of the State*, Cheltenham, UK and Northampton, MA, USA: Edward Elgar.
Chandler, A. (1962), *Strategy and Structure: Chapters in the History of the American Industrial Enterprise*, Cambridge, MA: MIT Press.
Chang, H-J. (2000), 'An institutionalist perspective on the role of the state: towards an institutionalist political economy', in L. Burlamaqui, A-C. Castro and H-J. Chang (eds), *Institutions and the Role of the State*, Cheltenham, UK and Northampton, MA, USA: Edward Elgar.
Coase, R.M. (1937), 'The nature of the firm', *Economica*, **4**: 386–405.
Coe, N., M. Hess, H.W. Yeung, P. Dicken and J. Henderson (2004), '"Globalising" regional development: a global production networks perspective', *Transactions of the Institute of British Geographers*, **29**(4): 468–84.
Cohen, M.D., R. Burkhart, G. Dosi, M. Egidi, L. Marengo, M. Warglien and S. Winter (1996), 'Routines and other recurring action patterns of organizations: contemporary research issues', *Industrial and Corporate Change*, **5**(3): 653–98.
Cohendet, P., P. Llerena and L. Simon (2010), 'The innovative firm: nexus of communities and creativity', *Revue d'Economie Industrielle*, **129–130**: 139–70.
Coriat, B. and O. Weinstein (2010), 'Les théories de la firme entre "contrats" et "compétences". Une revue critique des développements contemporains', *Revue d'Economie Industrielle*, **129–130**: 57–86.

Crotty, J. (2003), 'The neo-liberal paradox: the impact of destructive product market competition and impatient finance on non-financial corporations in the neo-liberal era', Political Economy Research Institute research brief no 5, University of Massachussetts Amherst.

Cullen, E. (2004), 'Unprecedented growth, but for whose benefits?', *FEASTA Review*, **2**: 9–43.

El Mouhoud, M. and D. Plihon (2009), *Le savoir et la finance. Liaisons dangereuses au cœur du capitalisme contemporain*, Paris: La découverte.

European Commission (2006), 'Putting knowledge into practice: a broad-based innovation strategy for the EU', COM(2006) 502 final, 13 September, Brussels.

European Commission (2010), 'Europe 2020. A strategy for smart, sustainable and inclusive growth', COM(2010) 2020, 3 March, Brussels.

Eurostat (2001), *Measuring the New Economy*, Luxembourg: Eurostat.

Eurostat (2008), *Statistics in Focus*, 37/2008, Luxembourg: Eurostat.

Fama, E. (1980), 'Agency problems and the theory of the firm', *Journal of Political Economy,* **88**: 288–307.

Fitoussi, J-P. and E. Laurent (2008), *La nouvelle écologie politique. Economie et développement humain*, Paris: Editions du Seuil et La République des Idées.

Fleischaker, S. (2004), *On Adam Smith's Wealth of Nations. A Philosophical Companion*, Princeton, NJ and Oxford: Princeton University Press.

Foss, N. (1997), *Firms and Strategy: A Reader in the Resource-based Approach*, Oxford: Oxford University Press.

Geanakoplos, J. and P. Milgrom (1985), 'A theory of hierarchies based on limited managerial attention', Cowles Foundation paper no.775, Yale University.

Gereffi, G. (1994), 'The organisation of buyer-driven global commodity chains: how US retailers shape overseas production networks', in G. Gereffi and M. Korzeniewicz (eds), *Commodity Chains and Global Capitalism*, Westport, CT: Praeger, pp. 95–122.

Government of Ireland (2008), 'Building Ireland's smart economy. A framework for sustainable economic revival', Department of the Taoiseach, Dublin.

Grant, R.M. (1996), 'Towards a knowledge-based theory of the firm', *Strategic Management Journal*, **17**, special issue 'Knowledge and the Firm': 109–22.
Greenan, N. and J. Mairesse (1999), 'Organisational change in French manufacturing: what do we learn from firm representatives and from their employees?', National Bureau of Economic Research working paper no. W7285.
Hirschman, A.O. (1999), *Crossing boundaries, selected writings*, Cambridge, MA: MIT Press.
Heinz, D.K. and N. Salvadori (2003), *Classical Economics and Modern Theory. Studies in Long-period Analysis*, London: Routledge.
International Monetary Fund (IMF) (2009), 'The state of public finance cross-country. Fiscal monitor: November 2009', IMF staff position note SPN/09/25, 3 November.
Jensen, M. and W. Meckling (1976), 'Theory of the firm: managerial behaviour, agency costs, and capital structure', *Journal of Financial Economics*, **3**: 305–60.
Kirby, P. (2010), *Celtic Tiger in Collapse. Explaining the Weaknesses of the Irish Model*, 2nd edn, Basingstoke: Palgrave Macmillan.
Kirkpatrick, G. (2009), 'The corporate governance lessons from the financial crisis', *Financial Market Trends*, **96**(1).
Labory, S. (1997), 'Firm structure and market structure in imperfectly competitive markets', PhD thesis, European University Institute, 21 February.
Labory, S. (2002), 'Relazioni tra grandi imprese e PMI. Considerazioni generali con particolare riferimento al settore moda', in *Il sistema moda in Toscana*, S. Labory and L. Zanni (eds), Florence: Collana IRPET.
Labory, S. and G. Prodi 'La creazione di vantaggi competitivi: nuovi ruoli per la politica industriale', in P. Bianchi and C. Pozzi (eds), *Le politiche industriali alla prova del futuro*, Bologna: Il Mulino.
Lehrer, M. and K. Asakawa (2004), 'Rethinking the public sector: idiosyncracies of biotechnology commercialization as motors of national R&D reform in Germany and Japan', *Research Policy*, **33**: 921–38.
Marengo, L. (1992), 'Coordination and organizational learning in the firm', *Journal of Evolutionary Economics*, **2**(4): 313–26.
Milberg, W. and D. Winkler (2009), 'Globalization, offshoring and

economic insecurity in industrialized countries', UN Department of Economic and Social Affairs working paper no. 87, ST/ESA/2009/DWP/87.

Nelson, R. and S. Winter (1982), *An Evolutionary Theory of Economic Exchange*, Cambridge, MA: Harvard University Press.

Nelson, R., W. Baumol and E. Wolff (1994), *Convergence and Productivity: Cross-National Studies and Historical Evidence*, Oxford: Oxford University Press.

O'Neill, J. and A. Stupaytskz (2009), Goldman Sachs global economics paper no. 192.

Organization for Economic Co-operation and Development (OECD) (2001a), *Beyond the Hype. The OECD Growth Project*, Paris: OECD.

OECD (2001b), 'Intangible investments, growth and policy', STI Directorate, DSTI/IND(2001), 5 September.

OECD (2003a), *The Policy Agenda for Growth. An Overview of the Sources of Economic Growth in OECD Countries*, Paris: OECD.

OECD (2003b), *The Sources of Economic Growth in OECD Countries*, Paris: OECD.

OECD, (2009), 'Corporate governance and financial crisis: key findings and main messages', OECD Steering Group on Corporate Governance, Paris: OECD, June.

Ohmae, K. (1995), *The End of the Nation-State: The Rise of Regional Economies*, New York: Simon & Schuster.

Osterman, P. (1994), 'How common is workplace transformation and who adopts it?', *Industrial and Labour Review*, **47**(2): 173–88.

Paija, L. (2000), 'Industrial network relationships in the Finnish ICT cluster', presentation at Organisation for Economic Co-operation and Development Cluster Focus Group Workshop 'Do Clusters Matter in Innovation Policy', Paris.

Penrose, E. (1959), *The Theory of the Growth of the Firm*, Oxford: Blackwell.

Pisani-Ferry, J. and J. Von Weizsäcker (2010), 'Exit strategies: How soon? How fast? How to coordinate? A European perspective on phasing out the emergency measures taken in response to the economic crisis', the German Marshall Fund of the US, Washington, accessed 9 November 2010 at www.gmfus.org/publications/index.cfm.

Prodi, R. (2008), *La mia visione dei fatti. Cinque anni di governo in Europa*, Bologna: Il Mulino.
Robbins, L. (1981), 'Economics and political economy', *American Economic Review, Papers and Proceedings*, **71**(2): 1–10.
Roberts, J. (2004), *The Modern Firm. Organizational Design for Performance and Growth*, Oxford: Oxford University Press.
Rodrik, D. (2008), *Nations et Mondialisations. Les stratégies nationales de développement dans un monde globalisé*, Paris: Editions La Découverte.
Rumelt, R.P. (1984), 'Towards a strategic theory of the firm', in R.B. Lamb (ed.), *Competitive Strategic Management*, Englewood Cliffs, NJ: Richard D. Irwin.
Sen, A. (1982), *Poverty and Famines: An Essay on Entitlement and Deprivation*, Oxford: Clarendon Press.
Smith, A. (1776), *An Inquiry into the Nature and Causes of the Wealth of Nations*, reprinted 1960 in two volumes, London: JM Dent & Sons Ltd.
Stiglitz, J. (2010), *Freefall: Free Markets and the Sinking of the Global Economy*, London: Allen Lane.
Sturgeon, T.J. (2008), 'From commodity chains to value chains: interdisciplinary theory building in an age of globalization', Sloan Industry Studies working paper WP-2008-2.
Sylos Labini, P. (2006), *Torniamo ai classici. Produttività del lavoro, progresso tecnico e sviluppo economico*, second reprint, Roma: Editori Laterza.
Välilä, T. (2006), 'No policy is an island: on the interaction between industrial and other policies', *EIB Papers*, **11**: 8–33.
Von Tunzelmann, N. (2010), 'Technology and technology policy in the post-war UK: "market failure" or "network failure"?', *Revue d'Economie Industrielle*, **129–130**, 237–58.
Wenerfeld, B. (1984), 'A resource-based view of the firm', *Strategic Management Journal*, **5**: 171–80.
Williamson, O. (1975), *Markets and Hierarchies: Analysis and Antitrust Implications*, New York: The Free Press.
Williamson, O. (1985), *The Economic Institutions of Capitalism*, New York: The Free Press.
Williamson, O. (1998), 'Transaction cost economics and organization theory', in G. Dosi, D.J. Teece and J. Chitry (eds), *Technology, Organization and Competitiveness: Perspectives on Industrial and Corporate Change*, Oxford: Oxford University Press.

Yeung, H.W. (2006), 'Situating regional development in the competitive dynamics of the global production networks: an East Asian perspective', The International Centre for the Study of East Asian Development working paper series no. 2006-15, Kitakyushu, Japan.

Index

11 September/Twin Towers disaster (2001) 20, 23, 24
2008 financial crisis 10–39 *see also* American economy *and* United States (US)
and gap between financial and productive spheres of the economy 33–8
reactions to 28–33 *see also* reactions to 2008 crisis

agency theory 75
Alchian, A. 75
Ali-Yrkkö 121
American economy (and) 16–17, 22, 23–8
banking losses in 25–6
banking reform measures 25 *see also* legislation (US)
chronology of crisis in 25–8
need for restructuring of 24–5
Asakawa, K. 90
Asia 136 *see also* China *and* India
consumer goods from 23
crises in 18
rapid growth in 21
rise in share of world exports in 42
unbundling in 43

Bacci, L. 48, 49
Bailey, D. 37, 40, 49, 50, 117
Baldwin, R. 6, 46, 47, 48, 49, 50, 142
bank(s)/banking institutions *see also* Germany
Bank of America 27
acquires Merrill Lynch 27
Bank of Canada 26
Bank of England 26
Bank of International Settlements 33
Bank of Switzerland 26
Barclays 35
Bear Sterns 26
Bear Sterns and JPMorgan 26–7, 35
Citibank 35
Citigroup 26
Crédit Suisse 35
European Central 26
Federal Reserve Bank of New York 26, 35
Goldman Sachs 26
HSBC Bank (USA) 25–6
Lehman Brothers 25, 26, 27, 35
Merrill Lynch 35
Northern Rock 26, 35
Société Générale 26, 35
UBS 26, 35
US Federal Reserve 26
Bangemann Report/approach 129, 133, 135
Berlin Wall 20, 29, 114, 136
Bianchi, P. 4, 20, 31, 50, 60, 91, 101, 124, 130
bipolar world/bipolarism 3, 11, 17, 20, 36, 40, 44, 114, 136
Black, S. 45
Brazil 3, 8, 11, 15, 28, 107–8, 112–13, 123
democratic government of 112
as example of balanced industrial development 112
Burlamaqui, L. 78
Business Cycles 14

Canton 21, 108–9
capabilities 7, 61, 77, 78, 99

concept of 105
domestic 117
strategic 73
capitalism 1, 8, 37, 63, 95, 140–41
  European 34–5, 125
  history of 13–14
  ruled by multi-level governance system 141
Chandler, A. 45
  U-form of 67
Chang, H.-J. 79–80
China 3, 8, 11, 15, 17, 22, 23, 28, 36, 37, 79, 96–8, 107–12, 123, 130
  see also Shenzhen
  cheap labour in 97
  and Deng Xsiao Ping 20, 109
  enters World Trade Organization 124
  entitlements and rights in 111
  growth obligations and liaison with US 111
  growth rates in 17–18, 20–21, 107–10
  and Guangdong 107, 108–9
  hukou regulations in 109
  imports less 43
  IT skills in 50
  as location for multinational production processes 49–50
  opening to world economy 20–21
  provisions and entitlements in 97–8
  rise in share of world exports 42, 43
Chinese syndrome: growth of provisions without entitlements 104
civil development 1, 2, 101, 137
  concept 82–3
climate change 81
  policies (Kyoto 1998) 98
Coase, R.M. 74
Coe, N. 59
Cohen, M.D. 78
Cohendet, P. 78
colonialism 14, 16–17
competition 2, 3, 45–8, 52, 57, 68, 70, 79, 83–5, 88, 97, 128, 133, 137, 140
  in banking sector 35
  fair 126, 127
  international 24, 46, 56
  policy 89, 99, 125, 129–30, 135
  worldwide 7, 36, 50–51
competitive advantage 3, 78
  sources of 85
competitiveness 4, 56, 78, 85, 120, 129, 143
  of European firms 127, 128, 135
  of Irish economy 116, 117
  international 135
  poles 53
Coriat, B. 74, 77, 78
corporate governance 36, 71
  efficiency of 90
  models of 34, 35
  problems 75
  regime in UK 93
  and separation of ownership and control 90
Cowling, K. 37, 40
crisis(es)
  of 2001–2 and 2008 132
  of Ancien régime 12
  and economic development (1945–2009) 12–18 *see also* economic development
  and macroeconomic evolution since the 1980s 18
  Greek and Latin roots of word 12
  history of (1945–1980s) 13–18
  reflection on the term 12–15
  use of the term 13
  warning signals of 18
Crotty, J. 34
Cullen, E. 116
Cyert, R.M. 77

Dahrendorf, R. 8, 94, 95–6, 98, 143
definitions of
  globalisation 37
  globalisation phenomenon 43
  industrial policy 1–2

Demsetz, H. 75
division of labour (and) 5, 7, 60–86, 140 *see also* industrial development *and* production organisation
  analysis of 61–70 *see also* labour productivity
  basis of productive efficiency 62–3
  production organisation: Smith's metaphor of pin factory 64–7
  scale economies 66–70 *see also main entry*
  British industrial revolution 96–7
  change in nature of work 5
  as determinant of wealth of nations 62
  determined by demand and competition 70
  as essence of the firm 78
  improvements in labour productivity 62
  market power, mobility and strategy 70–72
  and barriers to entry 70
  organised on global scale 99
  theoretical approaches to the firm 73–80 *see also main entry*
  two elements for 80–81

Economic Consequences of the Peace, The 15
Economic Co-operation and Development, Organization for (OECD) 51
  calls for transparent and monitored risk management (2009) 35
  recommends more transparency and control in corporate governance 36
  Steering Group on Corporate Finance (2009) 35
economic development 1, 5, 7, 83
  see also division of labour

key elements of 94–100 *see also* provisions and entitlements
  systemic failures in 6
economic monetary union (EMU) 32, 132 *see also* European Union
  and adoption of common currency 20
El Mouhoud, M. 33
emerging countries/economies 20, 37, 130
employees
  education for skilled 142
  fundamental labour rights of 98
  increase in stress for 142
  loss of work as result of offshoring 58
  short-term contracts for unskilled 142
entitlements 7, 8, 92, 103–4, 106–7, 110–12, 114–15, 117, 123, 135–6, 142 *see also* provisions and entitlements
entrepreneur(s)/ship 47–8, 57, 71, 74, 93, 122
Essays in Persuasion 15
European Coal and Steel Community 128
European Commission 51, 131–3, 138
  defines industrial policy as enterprise policy 137
  defines new approach to policymaking: 'open coordination method' 132
  proposes economic growth strategy 100
  reports on deindustrialisation in EU 130–31
European Community 8, 127–8
European Constitution, failure of ratification of 31
European Economic Community 17, 42
European experience, the 124–38
  see also industrial policy

economic opening and structural
  adjustment policies 124–5
and 'eurosclerosis' 128
European Union (EU) 8, 12, 35, 56,
  82, 123, 124 *see also* bank(s)/
  banking institutions *and*
  Lisbon Strategy
  and competitiveness gap between
    Japan and US 130
  defines European approach to
    industrial policy 133
  economic disparities within the
    33
  enlargement of 42
  framework programme and
    technology policy in 135
  negatively perceived by European
    citizens 133
  and new growth strategy (for
    2010 to 2020) 136–8
  human capital element of 137
  new members of 47
  and policy of promoting IT skills
    50
  primary industrial policy of 99
  as prototype of international
    coordination? 29–33
  and provisions and entitlements
    96
  as unable to agree on common
    fund 27

Fama, E. 75
Fannie Mae (Federal National
  Mortgage Association) 26, 27
financial markets, closure of 27
Finland 8, 107–8, 118–23
  consensus in 120
  control of interest rates in 119
  corporatism in 119
  as knowledge-based economy
    118, 120–21
  lack of entrepreneurship in 122
  and Nokia 121–2
  rapid industrialisation of 118–19
firm, the *see also* theoretical
  approaches to the firm
  competitiveness of 78
  Walrasian model of 74
Fitoussi, J-P. 8
Fleischaker, S. 142
flexible production system
  (designed by Ohno of Toyota)
  63
Fordist firms 71–2
Fordist production system 63, 66–7
foreign direct investment (FDI) 3,
  115–18
Foss, N. 77
France (and) 14, 16, 30, 127
  1950s approach to industrial
    policy 126
  family and state ownership in 35
  high tech cluster in Grenoble 56
  policy of 'competitiveness poles'
    53–4
  rise in share in world exports 42
  spending on rescuing savings
    banks 34
  strong interventionism 125
Freddie Mac (Federal Home Loan
  Mortgage Corporation) 26, 27

G-20 countries 28, 29
gap between financial and
  productive spheres of the
  economy 33–38
Gazard, P. 12
Geanakoplos, J. 75
General Motors production
  organisation (1920s) 67
*General Theory of Employment,
  Interest and Money, The* 16
Gereffi, G. 44
German(y) 28, 30, 128
  annual GDP in 33
  bank-firm relationships in 35
  banking crisis in 26
  creation of the Reich in 14
  fair function of markets in 127
  increases share of world exports
    42
  multinationals investing in
    Central and EE countries 29

policy to develop competence in biotechnologies 90
and rescue of IKB and Sachsenbank 35
global
   conflicts 14, 15
   economy 15, 140
   distribution network 57
   financial market 33
   GDP 28
   production networks 4, 59
global value chains 4, 6, 44–50, 52, 59, 60, 63, 130, 142, 143
globalisation (and) 3–4, 37 *see also* organisation of production
   change in access to fundamental rights 98
   clusters of SMEs 52–4
   impact on relationship between states and markets 140
   importance of 'territory' 52–4 *see also* small and medium enterprises (SMEs)
   increased competition 51, 68
   industrial policy – national or regional levels? 56–9
   knowledge-based economy 54–6
   phenomenon of 41–4
   regional change 59
   strategic coupling concept 59
Grant, R.M. 1996 78
Greece, crisis and deficit in 8, 31–2, 33, 132
Greenan, N. 45
Greenspan, A. 28, 35
gross domestic product (GDP) 4
   growth rates 18–20
   per capita 31

Heinz, D.K. 5
Hirschman, A.O. 138
Holland 27, 31
Hong Kong 21, 108, 109, 110
How to Pay for the War 16
human capital 7, 22, 49–50, 52–3, 59, 79, 88, 104, 105, 130, 135, 137, 141–2, 143

India 3, 11, 15, 17, 22, 37, 79, 97, 130
   IT skills in 50
   as location for multinational production processes 49–50
industrial development 60–86 *see also* division of labour; industrial policy *and* theoretical approaches to the firm
   four levers of 102–3
   key levers of 135–6
   sustainable 2, 82–3, 106, 122, 137
industrial policies as long-term strategies 106–23 *see also* Brazil; China; Finland; Ireland; Shenzhen *and* South Africa
industrial policy
   in the 1970s 127–8
   in the 21st century 130–31
   and the Bangemann Report/approach 129, 133
   constructivist 126
   failures and justification of 87
   four major levers for
      entitlements 7
      innovation 7
      resources (and human capital) 7
      territory 7
   framework for defining 87–105 *see also* economic development *and* state and the market
   frameworks for long-term vision 101–4, 134–6
   innovation and territory 101–2
   phases of evolution of European policy 134–5
   holistic approach to 6
   interventionist 125
   and the Lisbon Strategy 131–3
   in the Maastricht Treaty 129–30
   at national or regional levels 56–9 *see also* globalisation
   in a political economy framework 80–84

and provisions and entitlements 97, 102
in the Single European Act and Treaty on the European Union 128–30
sustainable 102
in the Treaty of Rome 126–7
as vision of industrial development 100–104
information and communication technology (ICT) 14, 119–21
see also Finland *and* Nokia
and IT revolution 46, 47
innovation(s) 7, 54–5, 85, 92–3, 101, 102–4, 106, 117, 121,123, 129, 130–32, 135–7, 141
capability 118
capacity 50
economic 55
as essential (dynamic) lever 135
European policy for 133
financial 10, 23, 36
policy/ies 87, 89, 93
product 38, 71, 79
and scale economies 69–70
as 'secrets' 85
as source of competitive advantage 85
intangible assets 4, 6–7, 48–9, 53, 69, 77, 141
growing importance of 50, 51–2, 84–6
International Accounting Standards Board 141
International Monetary Fund (IMF) 28, 95, 141
Ireland 8, 31, 32, 107–8, 115–18, 123
and 'Building Ireland's Smart Economy' (2008) 117
and foreign direct investment 115–16, 117
homelessness in 116
Small Business Operational Programme in 115
social failures in 116
weaknesses in economy of 115
Italy 30, 31

and fall in share of world exports 42
family/state ownership in 34, 35
industrial districts in 47–8, 55
and moving of production processes 47
restrictive fiscal policy of (2010) 133
Tuscany's leather districts in 49
unification of 14

Jäntti, M. 119, 120
Japan 17, 18, 28, 31, 72, 130
1997 crisis in 21
development of economy in 21
and Japanese 'disease' 21
loses market share to new players 97
Meiji revolution in 14
Ministry of International Trade and Industry (MITI) 125
and spending on bank rescues 34
unbundles to low-cost Asian countries 47
Jensen, M. 75

Keynes, J.M. 15–17, 18, 36
formulates proposal for Bancor (1943) 16
Kirby, P. 115, 116
Kirkpatrick, G. 35
Kondratiev, N.D. 13, 14
and Kondriatiev/long waves 13–14
Major Economic Cycles, The 13
knowledge content of products 50, 51
knowledge creation 104
and accumulation 143
process of the firm 142
knowledge management 51
knowledge-based economy 6, 31, 50, 51, 54–6, 57, 104, 118, 131, 136, 141 *see also* Finland
post-crisis 85
Korea/South Korea 15, 17, 130
Krugman, P. 18, 28

La crise de la conscience européene 12
Labini, S. 82, 83
Labory, S. 4, 20, 31, 47, 50, 72, 91, 101, 124, 130
labour legislation
 changes 98
 defined for unskilled 142
labour productivity 5
 as basis of productive efficiency 62–3
labour rights, fundamental 98
Latin America 18
 and *Decada Perdida* 22
Laurent, E. 8
League of Nations, failure of 15
legislation (European)
 Maastricht Treaty (1992) 129
 Single European Act (1986) 129
legislation (US)
 Dodd-Frank Wall Street Reform and Consumer Protection Act (2010) 25
 Glass-Steagall Act (1933, 1999) 25
 Economic Stimulus Act (2008) 26
 Housing and Economic Recovery Act (2008) 27
 Emergency Economic Stabilization Act (2008) 27
Lehman Brothers 25, 26, 27, 35
Lehrer, M. 90
Lewis-type dualism 117
Lisbon Strategy 82, 104, 124, 131–3, 136
 failure of 8, 31, 133
Lynch, L. 45

Maastricht Treaty 123, 129, 135
Mairesse, J. 45
managers 34–6, 45, 73, 78, 90
 high remuneration of 34
 stock options for 58
Mandela, N. 114
March, J.G. 77
Marengo, L. 77

market failure(s) 2, 77, 87, 88–91, 92, 100
 approach 83, 99
market power 51, 70–71, 89
market share(s) 97, 128
Meckling, W. 75
Milgrom, P. 75
Millberg, W. 58
Modern Social Conflict. An Essay on the Politics of Liberty, The 94
Monnet, J. 126

Nature of the Firm, The 74
Nelson, R. 77
neo-liberalism 92
 drawbacks of 36
 model of 36–7
 and short-term perspective flaw 36
Nixon, President R. 17
Nokia 121–2 *see also* Finland

Obama, President B. 25, 27
offshoring
 long-term effects of 58
 production phases to low-cost countries 58
 of routine tasks 48
Ohmae, K. 56
O'Neill, J. 3
organisation models
 constant improvement 72
 just-in-time 72
 modular production 72
organisation of production 5, 6–7, 38, 70, 83–5, 99, 141–2 *see also* unbundling
 and globalisation 40–59
 and global value chains 44–45
organisational competences 77
Osterman, P. 45
outsourcing 38, 41, 45–6

Paija, L. 120
Palmberg, C. 119
Penrose, E. 77

perspective
  long-term 36–7, 55, 58, 90, 122, 134, 139
  short-term 36, 37
Pisani-Ferry, J. 29
place leadership concept 50
Plihon, D. 33
product differentiation 67–8
production organisation
  of General Motors (1920s) 67
  and institutions and firm strategies 73
  M-form structure 67
  pin factory metaphor (Adam Smith) 64–7
production processes, Taylorist and Fordist 63
production system, modular 63
productive efficiency, specialisation and complementarity as basis of 62–3
provisions and entitlements 94–100, 110–12, 114–15, 117, 123, 135, 137, 140, 143
  as determining capacity to organise production 96–7
  and the EU 96
  and policies recommended by IMF/World Bank 95

reactions to 2008 crisis 28–33
  EU as prototype of international coordination 29–33 *see also main entry*
  fiscal stimulus measures 28–9
  tax cuts 28
  spending 28
research
  as feeding cultural growth 83
  needed on production processes 7
research and development 38, 51–2, 54, 58, 67, 71, 87, 90, 91, 116, 121, 123, 132, 137
resources 54, 68, 77, 82, 87, 94, 99, 101–4, 135, 139 *see also* human capital
Robbins, L. 3, 87, 92

Roberts, J. 73
Rodrik, D. 3, 8
Romania 47
  financial market closes in 27
Roosevelt, President 26
routine
  concept of 78
  depository of knowledge through 77
  tasks 48, 62
Rumelt, R.P. 77
Russia 3, 11, 15, 28, 120
  financial market closes in 27
  reasserts as world power 17

Salvadori, N. 5
scale economies 66–70
  and innovation 69–70
Schumpeter, J. 14, 141
Second World War 15
  reconstruction of economies after 16
Sen, A. 95, 103
Shenzhen 8, 21, 108–10
  critical issues for 110
  government of 110
  Stock Exchange 109
  universities in 110
Singapore 130
small and medium enterprises (SMEs) 47, 72
  clusters of 52–4, 55–6, 58
  EU strategy for 131
  and French policy of 'competitiveness poles' 53–4
  and poles of excellence 57, 58
  policies for 54–5, 57
  promotion of development of 129
Smith, A. 5, 7, 38, 57, 60, 61, 62–3, 68, 82, 84, 85, 88, 95, 108, 139, 140, 141
  metaphor of pin factory 64–6, 67
  and power of exchanging 70
South Africa 8, 96, 107–8, 113–15, 123
  and apartheid 114
  creation of Republic of 114

and entitlements 99, 114
unequal distribution of
  provisions in 114–15
specialisation 5, 45, 49, 62, 66
  of clusters 53, 56
  and complementarity 63, 72, 80, 85, 139
  of individuals 78–80
  task 53–4, 56
Stability and Growth Pact 32
state and the market (and) 88–94
  government failures 91–2
  market failures 88–91
  neo-liberal view 92
  systemic failures 92–4
Stiglitz, J. 8, 28
studies on
  identifying new waves in second half of 20th century 14
  increase in stress for workers 142
Stupnytskz, A. 3
Sturgeon, T.J. 46
surveys on
  changes in firms' organisation in France (Greenan and Mairesse, 1999) 45
  changes in firms' organisation in the UK (Osterman, 1994) 45
  changes in firms' organisation in the US (Black and Lynch, 1997) 45

Taiwan 130
Thailand 21–2
  and devolution of Thai currency 21
team production theory 75
territory 7, 47, 49, 54–5, 61, 63, 88, 91, 101–4, 106, 135, 136, 137
  importance of the 52–4
  theoretical approaches to the firm 73–80
  contractual and evolutionary 74
  evolutionary theory 77–80
  neoclassical view 74–5, 79, 82
  transaction cost theory 74, 75–7
Tract on Monetary Reform 15

transport costs 44, 46–7, 116
Treaty (of)
  Amsterdam 29
  Lisbon 31
  Nice 29
  Rome: Article 85(3) 127

Ukraine, financial market closes in 27
unbundling 44–52, 60, 92
  and growing importance of intangible assets 51–2, 84–6
  from last quarter of 20th century 46–7
  between late 19th and 20th centuries 46
  and organisation of production 44–51
  production internationalisation defined as 46
  second 6, 7, 46–7, 48, 51–2, 68, 80, 142 *see also* global value chains
United Kingdom (UK) 28, 42, 45
  corporate governance regime in 93
  crisis in 26, 30
  nationalisation of Northern Rock in 35
United Nations (UN) 98
United States (US) 28, 31 *see also* legislation (US)
  Barack Obama elected 27
  as biggest importing region 43
  Bureau of Labour Statistics 23
  and China 24–5
  economic problems in 23–8
  hegemony dominates post-World War II era 3
  Long Term Capital Management (LTCM) 27
  loss of market share to new players 97
  political unilateralism in 17
  Senate 25
  Treasury spending on rescue of savings banks 34

vulnerability of economy of 37
and Washington Consensus 17, 22, 130
United States Congress *see also* legislation (US)
   approves act to sustain economy (2009) 27
   rejects Paulson Plan 27

Välilä, T. 99, 100
value added chain 71–2
Vartiainen, V.J. 119, 120
Von Tunzelmann, N. 92–3
Von Weizsäcker, J. 29

Washington Consensus 17, 22. 130
Wealth of Nations The 5, 108

wealth of nations 1, 38, 60, 61, 95, 101, 139–40
   as 'civil development' 82
   determined by division of labour 7, 62–3
Weinstein, O. 74, 77, 78
Wenerfeld, B. 77
Williamson, O. 74, 75–6
Winkler, D. 58
Winter, S. 77
World Bank 95, 112
   and the Far East Miracle 21
World Trade Organization 124, 141

Yeung, H.W. 46, 59
Ylä-Antilla, P. 119